Domestic Violence

OPPOSING VIEWPOINTS®

D1248572

Domestic Violence

OPPOSING VIEWPOINTS®

Other Books of Related Interest

Domestic Violence

OPPOSING VIEWPOINTS®

David M. Haugen, *Book Editor*

Bruce Glassman, *Vice President*
Bonnie Szumski, *Publisher*
Helen Cothran, *Managing Editor*

**OPPOSING
VIEWPOINTS®
SERIES**

GREENHAVEN PRESS
An imprint of Thomson Gale, a part of The Thomson Corporation

THOMSON
━━━━✳━━━━ ™
GALE

Detroit • New York • San Francisco • San Diego • New Haven, Conn.
Waterville, Maine • London • Munich

LIBRARY OF CONGRESS CATALOGING-IN-PUBLICATION DATA

Domestic violence : opposing viewpoints / David M. Haugen, book editor.
    p. cm. — (Opposing viewpoints series)
Includes bibliographical references and index.
ISBN 0-7377-2224-X (lib. bdg. : alk. paper) —
ISBN 0-7377-2225-8 (pbk. : alk. paper)
    1. Family violence—United States. I. Haugen, David M., 1969– . II. Opposing viewpoints series (Unnumbered)
HV6626.2.D683 2005
362.82'92'0973—dc22   2004041168

"Congress shall make
no law...abridging the
freedom of speech, or of
the press."

First Amendment to the U.S. Constitution

The basic foundation of our democracy is the First
Amendment guarantee of freedom of expression.
The Opposing Viewpoints Series is dedicated to the
concept of this basic freedom and the idea that it is
more important to practice it than to enshrine it.

Contents

Why Consider Opposing Viewpoints?

"The only way in which a human being can make some approach to knowing the whole of a subject is by hearing what can be said about it by persons of every variety of opinion and studying all modes in which it can be looked at by every character of mind. No wise man ever acquired his wisdom in any mode but this."

John Stuart Mill

In our media-intensive culture it is not difficult to find differing opinions. Thousands of newspapers and magazines and dozens of radio and television talk shows resound with differing points of view. The difficulty lies in deciding which opinion to agree with and which "experts" seem the most credible. The more inundated we become with differing opinions and claims, the more essential it is to hone critical reading and thinking skills to evaluate these ideas. Opposing Viewpoints books address this problem directly by presenting stimulating debates that can be used to enhance and teach these skills. The varied opinions contained in each book examine many different aspects of a single issue. While examining these conveniently edited opposing views, readers can develop critical thinking skills such as the ability to compare and contrast authors' credibility, facts, argumentation styles, use of persuasive techniques, and other stylistic tools. In short, the Opposing Viewpoints Series is an ideal way to attain the higher-level thinking and reading skills so essential in a culture of diverse and contradictory opinions.

In addition to providing a tool for critical thinking, Opposing Viewpoints books challenge readers to question their own strongly held opinions and assumptions. Most people form their opinions on the basis of upbringing, peer pressure, and personal, cultural, or professional bias. By reading carefully balanced opposing views, readers must directly confront new ideas as well as the opinions of those with whom they disagree. This is not to simplistically argue that everyone who reads opposing views will—or should—change his or her opinion. Instead, the series enhances readers' understanding of their own views by encouraging confrontation with opposing ideas. Careful examination of others' views can lead to the readers' understanding of the logical inconsistencies in their own opinions, perspective on why they hold an opinion, and the consideration of the possibility that their opinion requires further evaluation.

Evaluating Other Opinions

To ensure that this type of examination occurs, Opposing Viewpoints books present all types of opinions. Prominent spokespeople on different sides of each issue as well as well-known professionals from many disciplines challenge the reader. An additional goal of the series is to provide a forum for other, less known, or even unpopular viewpoints. The opinion of an ordinary person who has had to make the decision to cut off life support from a terminally ill relative, for example, may be just as valuable and provide just as much insight as a medical ethicist's professional opinion. The editors have two additional purposes in including these less known views. One, the editors encourage readers to respect others' opinions—even when not enhanced by professional credibility. It is only by reading or listening to and objectively evaluating others' ideas that one can determine whether they are worthy of consideration. Two, the inclusion of such viewpoints encourages the important critical thinking skill of objectively evaluating an author's credentials and bias. This evaluation will illuminate an author's reasons for taking a particular stance on an issue and will aid in readers' evaluation of the author's ideas.

It is our hope that these books will give readers a deeper understanding of the issues debated and an appreciation of the complexity of even seemingly simple issues when good and honest people disagree. This awareness is particularly important in a democratic society such as ours in which people enter into public debate to determine the common good. Those with whom one disagrees should not be regarded as enemies but rather as people whose views deserve careful examination and may shed light on one's own.

11

Thomas Jefferson once said that "difference of opinion leads to inquiry, and inquiry to truth." Jefferson, a broadly educated man, argued that "if a nation expects to be ignorant and free . . . it expects what never was and never will be." As individuals and as a nation, it is imperative that we consider the opinions of others and examine them with skill and discernment. The Opposing Viewpoints Series is intended to help readers achieve this goal.

David L. Bender and Bruno Leone,
Founders

———————————

Greenhaven Press anthologies primarily consist of previously published material taken from a variety of sources, including periodicals, books, scholarly journals, newspapers, government documents, and position papers from private and public organizations. These original sources are often edited for length and to ensure their accessibility for a young adult audience. The anthology editors also change the original titles of these works in order to clearly present the main thesis of each viewpoint and to explicitly indicate the opinion presented in the viewpoint. These alterations are made in consideration of both the reading and comprehension levels of a young adult audience. Every effort is made to ensure that Greenhaven Press accurately reflects the original intent of the authors included in this anthology.

———————————

Introduction

"Despite the segmentation or balkanization of the field, there is one consensus that may have been reached. There is evidence that virtually every type and form of . . . intimate relationship has the potential of being violent."
—Richard J. Gelles, "Family Violence," in Robert L. Hampton, ed., Family Violence, *vol. 1, 1999.*

On June 15, 2003, the Family Violence Prevention Fund celebrated Father's Day with a nationwide campaign to honor men who have vowed to take a stand against domestic violence. Although recognizing the efforts of men to halt the spread of family violence is admirable, not everyone was pleased with the campaign. Several fatherhood organizations were appalled at the gesture. Others, like columnist Cathy Young, made the point: "Imagine a Mother's Day campaign that focused on stopping women's abuse of children." In a June 16 article for the *Boston Globe*, Young, who often decries male bashing in discussions of domestic violence issues, continued her complaint against the Family Violence Prevention Fund by noting:

> On the campaign's website, the organizers congratulate themselves on seeing men as not just "the problem" in domestic violence but a part of the solution. So far, so good. But the underlying approach is still one that assumes the perpetrators are men and the victims are women, ignoring the complex picture of family violence that emerges from nearly three decades of research.

The three decades of research that Young refers to began with a National Institute of Mental Health study conducted in 1977 by Murray Straus and Richard Gelles. A domestic violence survey was sent to over two thousand couples in the United States. The authors followed up the initial research with a second survey in 1985 sent to six thousand couples (married and cohabitating) across the nation. From their results, Straus and Gelles determined that men and women were equally apt to resort to minor incidents of violence (shoving, slapping, throwing objects) in domestic disputes.

However, in more severe incidents of violence (kicking, hitting with a fist, threatening with or using a knife or gun), the survey revealed that women were more likely to be the perpetrators and not the victims.

Men's organizations defend these findings because they counter the common assumption that domestic violence is a gendered issue, specifically one in which men are prone to violence in order to retain their power in the family and in society as a whole. The Fatherhood Coalition, a Massachusetts-based men's rights organization, insists that most laws relating to domestic violence unfortunately adhere to this assumption despite evidence to the contrary. According to one of the coalition's guiding principles, "All efforts to address domestic violence that ignore female aggression must be challenged whenever possible. Any and all laws that are written to protect one class of adults at the expense of the civil rights of another class are reprehensible in nature and antithetical to the principles of liberty and equal protection on which our nation was founded."

Nancy Scannell, legislative director of Jane Doe, Inc., a Massachusetts-based domestic violence coalition, disputes the notion that men are equally victimized by domestic violence. In a 2002 *Boston Globe* article, Scannell argues: "Men are sometimes victims of domestic violence, but the attempt to be inclusive [of male victims] should never be interpreted to mean that the issue is gender-neutral. It does not change our mind about why [domestic violence] happens. It happens because of sexism and power and control of men over women in our society."

The National Coalition Against Domestic Violence (NCADV) agrees with Scannell that power and control are at the root of domestic abuse. Their website contains a section entitled "Why Do Men Batter Women?" that profiles common traits of a batterer:

- A batterer objectifies women. He does not see women as people. He does not respect women as a group. Overall, he sees women as property or sexual objects.

- A batterer has low self-esteem and feels powerless and ineffective in the world. He may appear successful, but inside he feels inadequate.

- A batterer externalizes the causes of his behavior. He blames his violence on circumstances such as stress, his partner's behavior, a "bad day," alcohol or other factors.

The batterer in this case is obviously male, but it is noteworthy that the NCADV website does not contain a section on female batterers. The NCADV, like Scannell, operates from the theory that men are the primary perpetrators of domestic abuse.

This argument is well supported. The majority of statistical evidence finds that most reported domestic violence incidents involve women victims. The 1998 National Crime Victimization Survey (NCVS) concluded that 85 percent of victims were women. The NCVS also reported that half of those female victims had sustained injuries, whereas only 32 percent of male victims of domestic violence had acknowledged any injuries. Of those people killed by violent partners, 72 percent were women. The disparity in these last two statistics is typically attributed to the greater average physical strength of men.

Those who defend Straus's and Gelles's claims, however, maintain that greater physical strength does not equate to a brutish nature, nor does it dismiss the fact that women also have the ability to be extremely violent. According to the National Family Violence Survey (first issued in 1975), the rate of severe assaults by men in the home has dropped by 50 percent—from thirty-eight per one thousand couples to twenty. The rate of severe assaults by women in the home has remained static at nearly forty-five per one thousand couples over that time period. In 2001, twenty-two-year-old Amanda DaCosta killed her thirty-eight-year-old former boyfriend, Jeffrey Smith, by stabbing him in the heart. DaCosta's defense attorney initially planned to portray his client as a battered woman seeking a way out of a violent relationship. It was quickly revealed, however, that no record of abuse existed and DaCosta had caught Smith in bed with another woman at the time of the stabbing.

The so-called battered woman defense is one of the common explanations that women's advocates give for domestic violence incidents in which the male partner is killed. According to this plea, the woman, so dominated and abused by her partner, either lashes out fiercely enough in a time of desperation to actually kill her partner or plans the homicide as the only conceivable means of escaping the relationship. Some critics of this defense, however, note that it never seems to be applied to cases in which men are accused of domestic murder. Mark Charalambous, a spokesman for the Fatherhood Coalition, argues that law enforcement and the court system are designed around the belief that men are the perpetrators of domestic violence. In a 2002 letter to the editor of the *Fitchburg* (Massachusetts) *Sentinel & Enterprise*, Charalambous asserts, "The notion that men may in fact be defending themselves when they are charged with domestic violence, or that the woman may simply be lying is never considered."

Given the prevalence of female victims in abuse cases, it is easy to understand the argument that domestic violence is a gendered issue. However, men's advocacy groups, point out that the risk in doing so may leave male victims without a voice. Other subsections of the population, such as gay men and lesbians, also believe that the definition of the issue should be broad enough to encompass abusive relationships within their communities. For this reason, many researchers favor casting the issue in more inclusive terms. Eve S. Buzawa and Carl G. Buzawa in their book on domestic violence state: "Although injuries due to violence occur disproportionately against women, and men commit more serious violent acts, both genders engage in violence." Because of this fact, the Buzawas favor terminology such as *domestic violence* since it emphasizes that "any domestic violence is inappropriate, regardless of gender."

The controversy over the gendering of domestic violence is just one of the many debates examined in *Opposing Viewpoints: Domestic Violence*. Noted researchers, clinicians, and pundits in this anthology explore other topics in the following chapters: Is Domestic Violence a Serious Problem? What Causes Domestic Violence? Are Legal Remedies Effective in Curbing Domestic Violence? and How Can Social Services Reduce Domestic Violence? As these chapter titles suggest, the viewpoints in this anthology examine not only the prevalence of domestic violence but also the criminal justice and social service response to the problem.

CHAPTER 1

Is Domestic Violence a Serious Problem?

Chapter Preface

In February 2003, the Department of Justice released updated findings for its most recent National Crime Victimization Survey (NCVS). The NCVS gathers information on crime victimization from forty-two thousand households in the United States. According to the updates, there were an estimated 691,710 nonfatal violent crimes caused by an intimate partner in 2001. Roughly 85 percent of those domestic crimes involved women victims. Additionally, just over 1,200 women and 440 men were killed by intimate partners in 2000, the last year for which estimates on domestic murder are available. Overall, these numbers reveal a decline in the rates of domestic violence since 1993. Between that year and 2001, intimate violence against women fell by nearly 50 percent. Within the same period, intimate violence against men dropped 42 percent.

Some analysts point to the NCVS data as proof that domestic violence is not a serious crime in the United States. Although by no means dismissing the problem or its terrible consequences, these critics maintain that relative to other crimes, domestic violence is not widespread. For example, in 2002, the Department of Justice reported that there were roughly 23 million crimes in the nation. Of these, 23 percent were crimes of violence; and of that number, about 20 percent were nonfatal violent crimes against women and around 3 percent were nonfatal violent crimes against men. This number is half the number of robberies in the country, and far lower than the number of simple or aggravated assaults that occur each year.

On the other hand, all of the percentages translate into more than 1 million women and 150,000 men who suffered domestic abuse in 2002. Victims, advocates, and law enforcement view these numbers as staggering. To them, the trend in violence may be declining, but both the higher rates in the past as well as current statistics illustrate how deeply rooted domestic violence is in American society. Furthermore, various subgroups hidden within these figures want to make sure that analysts recognize that the percentages are not evenly spread across the nation's demographics. African

American women, for example, are victimized at a rate 35 percent higher than that of white women. Similarly, homosexual men and women do not want their experiences denied by a false assumption that domestic violence applies only to heterosexual relationships.

The NCVS, however, is only one statistical measure of domestic violence. The authors of the viewpoints in the following chapter use various crime statistics and personal experiences to debate the extent and severity of the problem in the United States.

"At one time [domestic violence] was considered the most dangerous police call; now it is generally accepted as the most frequent form of violence in the United States."

Domestic Violence Is a Serious Problem

Denise Kindschi Gosselin

A police officer and frequent lecturer, Denise Kindschi Gosselin argues that domestic violence has reached epidemic proportions in the United States. In this selection from her book *Heavy Hands: An Introduction to the Crimes of Domestic Violence*, Gosselin claims that domestic violence is still the most frequent type of violence reported to the police. The high volume of reports reveals that this crime cuts across race, ethnicity, social status, and age. All women, according to Gosselin, are more likely to be injured or killed in bouts of domestic violence than in vehicle accidents, rapes, and muggings combined. Domestic violence also involves battered husbands, abused partners in homosexual relationships, and younger people affected by dating violence and acquaintance rape. Because domestic violence impacts so many people, Gosselin regards it as a major social problem that cannot be ignored.

As you read, consider the following questions:

1. According to Gosselin, husbands and boyfriends were responsible for the death of what percentage of female murder victims?
2. How old is the average abuser, as reported by the author?

Denise Kindschi Gosselin, *Heavy Hands: An Introduction to the Crimes of Domestic Violence*. Upper Saddle River, NJ: Prentice-Hall, 2000. Copyright © 2000 by Pearson Education, Inc. Reproduced by permission.

Domestic violence is the single most frequent violence that police officers encounter, according to [a 1992 study by] Lawrence Sherman. Police respond up to 8 million times per year to violence that involves a spouse or lover. At one time it was considered the most dangerous police call; now it is generally accepted as the most frequent form of violence in the United States.

A Major Social Problem

The battered woman is by far the most frequent victim of domestic violence. She is typical of any woman that you encounter in public, but the danger for her is in her own home. She comes from every walk of life, every age, race, ethnicity, and social class. Women's battering has reached epidemic proportions in the United States and is considered a major social problem. Domestic violence is the leading cause of injury and death to American women, causing more harm than vehicular accidents, rapes, and muggings combined. Although many expect domestic violence victims to be poor, uneducated women, the picture is inaccurate. Their partners victimize many professional women. This is true even though a number of the female victims earn more money than their abusers earn. According to the Commonwealth Fund 1998 Survey of Women's Health: "One of six women experienced physical and/or sexual abuse during childhood. The equivalent of three million women nationwide reported experiencing domestic abuse in the past year. Nearly two in five women had at some point been physically or sexually assaulted or abused, or had been a victim of domestic violence in their lifetime. One in five said she had been raped or assaulted in her lifetime."

Murderous Relationships

Each year, an estimated 30 percent of women who become homicide victims die at the hands of men with whom they have a family. Husbands or boyfriends killed 28 percent of female murder victims in 1994. Many people fault the battered woman who does not leave her abuser. Yet women do leave abusive relationships. It is at the time of separation that the women are most vulnerable to being beaten and killed.

Women who leave their abusive partners are at greater risk of being killed, up to 75 percent greater than for those who stay. A woman is most likely to be murdered when trying to break off an abusive relationship.

Abuse of pregnant women is the leading cause of birth defects and infant mortality, according to the March of Dimes. Lenore Walker has reported a high degree of battering during first, second, and third pregnancies. Determining the extent of marital rape is complicated by the fact that some states still do not legally recognize marital rape, while others have extended their definitions to include cohabitors. Walker has also found a strong correlation between marital rape and battered women; 59 percent of her sample stated that they were forced to have sex with their spouses. Studies have indicated that as many as 1 in 10 wives may have been sexually assaulted by their spouses at least once. The majority of domestic violence perpetrators have prior criminal records, according to numerous National Institute of Justice studies. A Minneapolis study in 1984 found that 60 percent of domestic violence abusers had prior criminal records. In 1992, [David J.] Hirschel reported finding 79 percent of domestic abusers were criminals. Consistent with these findings, a large study conducted in Massachusetts found that 78 percent of men brought before the court for restraining orders in 1990 had at least one prior criminal complaint, the average being 13. The majority of offenders in the Massachusetts study had already been prosecuted for failing to obey a court or Registry of Motor Vehicle injunction. The implication is that many domestic violence perpetrators have indicated through prior legal proceedings that they are inclined toward noncompliance. This finding is problematic since the primary response of the court is to protect the domestic violence victim through court order. The average abuser brought to police attention is 32 years old, with two-thirds between their mid-20s and early 40s.

Husband Battering

Some researchers suggest that the incidence of male battering may be as high as female battering. Most experts, however, typically accept the incidence rate of male battering by females to be approximately 5 percent of domestic violence. [Suzanne K.] Steinmetz first reported the problem as the *battered husband syndrome* in 1978. Two national surveys conducted in 1975 and 1985 by [Murray A.] Straus and [Richard J.] Gelles suggest that domestic violence by women is increasing and violence by men is decreasing. An earlier study indicated that spousal abuse is almost gender-neutral in most categories of violence. [In 1996] Straus reiterated that every study of married and cohabiting couples that was not self-selective found a rate of assault by women on male partners to be the same as the rate of assault by men on female partners.

Estimates of Domestic Violence

Violence among current and former intimate partners is pervasive in American society. Every year an estimated 8.7 million women are abused by their partners. Two national studies have provided methodologically rigorous national estimates of the prevalence of woman battering. [P.] Tjaden and [N.] Thoennes's (2000) National Violence Against Women Survey was based on a national representative sample of 8,000 women and 8,000 men 18 years of age and older. The report based on this study indicated that almost 25% of the women surveyed and 7.6% of the men stated in telephone interviews that they had been raped and/or physically battered by a spouse, cohabiting partner, or date during their lifetime; 1.5% of the women surveyed indicated that they had been physically abused or raped by an intimate partner during the previous 12-month period. A study by [M.A.] Straus and [R.J.] Gelles (1991) was based on a national representative sample of 5,349 couples and 3,334 children. Based on self-reports, Straus and Gelles estimated that approximately 16% of American couples had encountered family violence incidents such as punching, kicking, and assaults with a heavy object or a weapon. This estimate results in approximately 8.7 million battered women annually, based on the U.S. population of couples. However, these estimates are likely to be gross underestimates because of underreporting.

Albert R. Roberts, "Duration and Severity of Woman Battering: A Conceptual Model/Continuum," in Albert R. Roberts, ed., *Handbook of Domestic Violence Intervention Strategies: Policies, Programs, and Legal Remedies*. New York: Oxford University Press, 2002.

The prevalence of husband battering is an issue of considerable controversy. Some researchers altogether deny the existence of a battered husband syndrome. Because the acknowledgment of a male syndrome would be in contrast to the theoretical explanations for wife battering, the position may be a legitimate one. Feminist theorists suggest that it detracts from the importance of the immense problem of female battering. Law enforcement officers, however, would disagree. There is reluctance by law enforcement to arrest female perpetrators, indicating a smaller percentage of perpetrators than in reality. The Kenosha Domestic Abuse Intervention Project indicated that after institution of a domestic violence mandatory arrest law, women exhibited a 12-fold increase in arrests relative to pre-mandatory arrest compared to a twofold increase for men during the same period. The author of the project cautions that women and men do differ in their rate of violence and that self-defense is most often the underlying cause for domestic violence by females.

Precursors

Often cited as a precursor to spouse abuse, dating violence and acquaintance rape have received considerable national attention lately. The sexual climate on college campuses has been identified as nothing less than treacherous for women. As reported by [Louis] Copeland and [Leslie R.] Wolfe:

- In a survey of 3,187 college women, 478 reported having been raped; of these, 10.6 percent were raped by strangers; 24.9 percent were raped by nonromantic acquaintances; 21 percent were raped by casual dates; and 30 percent were raped by steady dates.
- More than half of college rape victims had been attacked by dates.
- Studies of high school and college students conducted during the 1980s reported rates of dating violence ranging from 12 to 65 percent.

For incidents other than rape, a number of studies have confirmed that females self-report a higher incidence of violence toward men than do men toward women in their dating relationships. A study in 1991 indicated that female college students were more likely than males to resort to using violence to control, show anger, or retaliate for emotional hurt.

Vallerie Coleman has recently demonstrated that lesbian

violence is a significant problem, noting the reluctance by both lesbians and mainstream society to recognize violence between women. In *Domestic Partner Abuse* she reviews the available literature and concludes that "the prevalence and severity of lesbian battering are comparable to that of heterosexual relationships . . . rates of violence in lesbian relationships ranging from 25% to 48%." Coleman cites a [1989] study that compared rates of violence among couples that were heterosexual, lesbian, and gay. No significant differences in prevalence were found in partner abuse; heterosexual couples evidenced the lowest rate of abuse, at 28 percent; gay men had a rate of 38 percent; and lesbian couples had the highest rate, 48 percent.

Another form of intimate violence, gay domestic violence, is slowly coming to the surface. This form of violence is difficult to determine due to societal preconceptions about a battered victim. We expect that one will be larger and stronger than the other. Frequently, we view battering between men as normal aggressive behavior. Issues in gay relationships are forcing us to reconceptualize domestic violence. Battered gay and bisexual victims often respond to battering by striking back, which also occurs in male-female relationships. Typically, this attempt at self-protection is mutual physical aggression. When the perpetrator and victim are roughly of the same physical size and strength, the violence is misperceived as "mutual."

Children Against Parents

Of all forms of domestic violence, this one is the least known of all: children battering their parents. How much battering goes on can be left to one's imagination. Parents who are physically or sexually assaulted will rarely report their child. It is a source of shame and confusion. Statistics on the numbers of parents that are killed by their adolescent children have been documented. Between 1977 and 1986, the killing of a parent was an almost daily event in the United States, with over 300 parents killed each year.

[Kathleen M.] Heide conducted an in-depth analysis of the FBI Supplementary Homicide Report data for this period, which revealed that parents and stepparents murdered were typically white and non-Hispanic. Further, in the majority of cases, the child who killed was also a white, non-Hispanic male. More than 70 percent of those killing fathers, stepfathers, or stepmothers were under 30 years of age, while almost 70 percent of those killing mothers were between 20 and 50. Sons and daughters under age 18 killed 15 percent of murdered mothers, 25 percent of fathers, 30 percent of stepmothers, and 34 percent of stepfathers.

"The crime of domestic violence is a small mark on the tableau of American criminal justice."

Domestic Violence Is Not a Serious Problem

Charles E. Corry

In the following viewpoint, Charles E. Corry claims that domestic violence is not a prevalent crime in the United States. Using other researchers' analysis of statistics from the National Crime Victimization Survey (NCVS), a biannual survey administered by the Census Bureau on behalf of the Department of Justice, Corry infers that between 150,000 and 340,000 violent domestic crimes occurred in 1994. Although he maintains that this is not an insignificant number, it is roughly one-twentieth of the number of simple assaults and one-eighth the number of aggravated assaults reported by the NCVS in 1994. More disheartening to Corry are the fictitious statistics reported by feminist groups that would lead one to believe that domestic violence is a far more widespread crime. Corry argues that such groups inflate the statistics in order to demonize men. Corry is the president of the Equal Justice Foundation, a nonprofit organization concerned with maintaining the rule of law and a social order that treats all people equitably.

As you read, consider the following questions:

1. Why does Corry insist that it is common sense to recognize that the NCADV estimates of domestic violence are fabricated?
2. According to Corry, what is "conspicuously absent" from feminist literature on domestic violence?

There is a national crusade to stop domestic violence [DV] and abuse, a seemingly noble goal for the new millennium. Everyone can support the abolition of domestic abuse as it involves gun control, prohibition of drugs and alcohol, getting tough on crime, social engineering, sexual prohibitions, creation of a vast bureaucracy for "victim" assistance, etc. In fact, just about any radical group, left or right, that you want to name has a stake in enacting laws prohibiting violence against women. But what is the real magnitude of the problem? Who are the victims? And who really is responsible for violence within families and couples?

The NCVS Survey

As best we can tell domestic violence is quite a rare crime. The National Crime Victimization Survey (NCVS) has been collecting data on personal and household victimization of intimate partners since 1973 in an ongoing survey of a nationally representative sample of residential addresses.

While there are limitations and biases in the data collected, the NCVS is a primary source of information on characteristics of all types of criminal victimization, and on the number and types of crimes *not* reported to law enforcement authorities as well as those that are.

The NCVS provides the largest national forum for *victims* to describe the impact of crime and the characteristics of violent offenders.

Twice each year data are obtained from a sample of roughly 49,000 households encompassing about 100,000 individuals on the frequency, characteristics, and consequences of criminal victimization in the United States. Thus, there is no more authoritative source than the NCVS as to what crimes *victims* are encountering in their lives.

It is of fundamental importance to understand that the NCVS data are not taken from police statistics or social surveys, and do not count couples who have bitter or loud arguments, a push-and-shove situation, S&M, or other aberrations couples may engage in. The NCVS is a survey of citizens who believe a crime has been committed in their household whether or not the crime was reported to police or any other authorities.

A Small Percentage

Current societal concern for domestic violence dates from 1971 when Erin Pizzey opened the first refuge (shelter in the U.S.) for battered women in Chiswick, London, England. [D.A.] Gaquin (1977–78) examined the first available NCVS data after 1971 on the crime of domestic violence. For the years 1973–1975 he found an extremely low rate of intimate partner violence of 2.2 incidents per 1,000 couples, or 0.22%.

Twenty years later, after domestic violence had been brought to worldwide attention on a constant, if not hysterical basis, [L.] Dugan (2003) examined the NCVS data from January 1992 to June 1998 for 529,829 households in the United States. She reports: "From those, 2,873, or 0.5%, reported at least one incident of domestic violence (unweighted)."

As we are constantly reminded of a "cycle of violence" in domestic abuse cases there is also the question of how often incidents of violence are repeated in a household. Dugan reports that for the same interval the NCVS data show a total of 3,508 incidents of criminal domestic violence in the 2,873 households reporting such violence. So at most 20% reported repetitive criminal acts of domestic violence, or <0.1% of the surveyed households.

There were an estimated 68.5 million family households in 1994 (Statistical Abstracts of the United States, 1997), the midpoint of Dugan's compilation. If we extrapolate from the NCVS data, and assume that 0.5% of those households had at least one incident of criminal domestic violence, there would have been about 340,000 cases in that year. That after twenty years of intense bombardment by radical feminist propaganda claiming all men are "batterers" and all women are "victims" of domestic violence.

Given the intense propaganda about DV between 1971 and 1994, the figure of 0.22% given by Gaquin might be a better benchmark. That would suggest about 150,000 cases of criminal domestic violence in the entire United States in 1994.

The 340,000 DV crimes in 1994 derived from Dugan's review is not an insignificant number but it is certainly far fewer cases of criminal domestic violence than we are led to believe by radical feminists and social studies, and hardly sufficient to generate and support the current hysteria about battered women. To put the crime of domestic violence, primarily assaults, in perspective we need to compare it with similar crimes. In 1994 there were an estimated 6,650,000 simple assaults and 2,478,000 aggravated assaults based on the NCVS data.

Without making any judgements regarding the societal interest in the topic of domestic violence one would be forced to conclude that, according to victims surveyed by the NCVS, the crime of domestic violence is a small mark on the tableau of American criminal justice. . . .

Imaginary Statistics

In stark contrast with the NCVS data the Denver-based National Coalition Against Domestic Violence (NCADV) [an organization dedicated to the empowerment of battered women and their children] estimates in their general information packet that: "Over 50% of all women will experience physical violence in an intimate relationship, and for 24–30% of those women the battering will be regular and on-going." If their statistics were valid, and you are not beating your wife, then the guy next-door must be beating his at least occasionally. And the woman living with the guy two or three doors down is getting beaten at least once a month.

Common sense alone, an uncommon virtue in the domestic violence debate, tells us the NCADV statistics are an outrageous fabrication. Also, if you talk to your male friends about domestic abuse we think they will know of a few instances of abused women, but are likely to know many more men whose female partners have abused them both physically and mentally, as well as abusing the law by bringing false allegations of domestic violence or abuse against them.

[Parenting expert and author] Armin Brott asked the NCADV where their statistics came from and got the following:

> Rita Smith, the group's coordinator, told [him] these figures were only "estimates." From where? "Based on what we hear out there." Out where? "Battered women's shelters and other advocacy groups."

In one of their "fact sheets," the National Coalition Against

Domestic Violence tells us that women who leave their batterers "increase by 75% their chances of getting killed." When I asked her to explain that figure, the NCADV's Rita Smith admitted that statistic isn't true at all, and that the Coalition has no concrete evidence of the effect—if any—leaving a violent partner will have on a woman. I then asked Ms. Smith whether it bothered her that her organization was responsible for spreading an imaginary statistic. "Not really," she said. "We think the chance of getting killed goes up and we're just trying to make a point here."

Asking women at a shelter, or victims of battering whether they've been hit, is like asking patrons at McDonald's whether they ever eat fast food. Ask *your* friends if one out of every four women they know is regularly battered as implied by these statistics? It would appear that the people who ten years ago were telling us that 50,000 children a year were disappearing in the United States have now found other work.

Feminist Misinformation

Such problems arise with any agencies that work with traumatized clients and that are trying to create a democratic organizational structure. Women's services tend to go the extra mile, attempting to create services consistent with *their* vision of how society should be structured to eliminate the problems their clients face (abuse, violence, sexism, racism, poverty, etc.). By doing so they often become polarized.

By far the worst distortion of the numbers of battered women comes from Miami talk show host Pat Stevens, who appeared on a segment of CNN's *Crossfire* show called "OJ on the Air." Stevens estimated that when adjusted for under reporting, the true number of battered women is 60 million. No one bothered to tell Stevens—or *Crossfire's* millions of viewers—that 60 million is more than 100% of all the women in the United States who are currently in relationships with a man. Instead, Stevens' "estimate" and the other "facts" on battered women all serve to fuel the claims that there is an "epidemic of domestic violence" and a "war against women."

All this says nothing about women attacking or provoking men. For the Denver-based National Coalition Against Domestic Violence (NCADV) ". . . the risk factor for battering is being born female." However, numerous investigators have

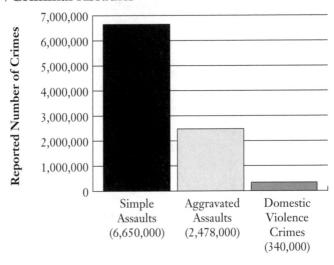

Comparing Domestic Violence to Other Criminal Assaults

Reported Number of Crimes

7,000,000
6,000,000
5,000,000
4,000,000
3,000,000
2,000,000
1,000,000
0

Simple Assaults (6,650,000)

Aggravated Assaults (2,478,000)

Domestic Violence Crimes (340,000)

Type of Crime

1994 Crime Statistics Extrapolated from NCVS Data.

pointed out that the risk factor isn't in being born a woman. The risk is in a woman living with a very dangerous animal, the human male. Provoking a male, at any time or any place, for any reason, is always risky, as any man will tell you. And in examining the influences of race, ethnicity, gender, and place, [J.L.] Lauritsen and [N.A.] White (2001) state that: ". . . the proportion of households with children that are female-headed was the strongest and most consistent community predictor of risk for all forms of violence."

However, to further their cause, in May, 1999, the NCADV sponsored their 1st Annual Kick-Boxing Marathon, which is in line with the feminist mantra: "For women, violence is a necessary resource for self-protection." In other words, violence is good if a woman employs it, but a crime if a man uses it, even in self defence or for the defence of others.

What Has Been Left Out

There is a conspicuous absence from the feminist literature about women who abuse their male partners. When such references are made, the women are characterized as "self defenders." [Author and skeptic] Robert Sheaffer has reviewed Denver-psychologist Lenore Walker's book on *The Battered Woman* that forms the basis for many of the present domestic violence and abuse laws in Colorado and the United States. Among many other shortcomings of her book, he notes that:

> *The Battered Woman* is unsatisfactory as a serious work, and completely unacceptable as a foundation for family law. First, it is profoundly unscholarly. Without objective verification of the incidents herein described, they are nothing more than hearsay. Second, the book does not even pretend to be objective: the woman's side, and only the woman's side, is presented, when it is undeniable that in a large percentage of cases, the woman initiates violence against the man. Third, Prof. Walker's expanded definition of "battering" that includes verbal abuse does not even address the issue of female verbal abuse of men. Fourth, there is no reason whatsoever to believe that Prof. Walker's sample of "battered women" is in any way a representative sample, and even if it were, she presents no statistics to support her conclusions. In fact, most of her conclusions are utterly unsupported by any kind of hard data, and are simply pronounced *ex cathedra*.

[Political activist] Richard Bennett has also looked at Ms. Walker's background and notes that:

> . . . some very odd things were happening in Denver, Colorado. A husband and wife team, Morton Flax and Lenore Walker, opened a family therapy practice dealing with abusive couples. Though Lenore, a Doctor of Education, was not really able to carry her end of the deal intellectually, they developed, with guidance from Ms. Pizzey of Chiswick, an innovative protocol for re-directing violent couples, which they practiced until Flax shot himself. *People close to the couple have described Dr. Flax as a "battered man."* [Emphasis added]

Her husband's suicide left Walker high and dry, and she drowned her sorrows in writing. She published in 1979 her best-seller, *The Battered Woman*, reaching a much broader audience than lesbian Del Martin with *The Battered Wife* in 1976, and Pizzey had with her 1974 classic, *Scream Quietly or the Neighbors Will Hear*, published in the UK.

Walker's book is more a self-help manual than a work of empirical science, as it relies exclusively on anecdotal reports from battered women themselves. At no time after the death of Dr. Flax has Walker worked with men, so the family violence community was understandably shocked when she agreed to work with the OJ Dream Team as an expert witness on Abusive Men. She's a woman's therapist, period.

For more accurate views of violent women than Lenore Walker, we suggest Erin Pizzey's book *Prone to Violence*, re-released in 1998 as *The Emotional Terrorist and the Violence Prone*, or the *When She Was Bad* book by Patricia Pearson.

There is also the broader question of whether or not a woman is ever assaulted in her relationship with a man. [D.G.] Dutton cites surveys by female interviewers of female respondents using strategies to maximize disclosure. About 12% reported an act that could be regarded as *severe violence at any time* during their marriage. About 28% reported some *minor violence*, e.g., pushing or a slap, at some time during their entire relationship.

The Revs. Sam and Bunny Sewell provide a detailed report on the misuse of statistics where they point out that:

> . . . It suits the political agenda of feminists to quote statistics that make men look bad. Most of the feminist empire depends on their success in demonizing men. The term "family violence" is familiar to professionals and is inclusive of violent females. Feminists began to use the term "domestic violence" while quoting arrest statistics that emphasized male abusers and female victims. This was necessary so the public focus would be on the only police statistics that made their scam look believable. Con artists call this the "hook."

> *"The truth is, women are just as violent as men and commit severe acts of violence against their partners almost twice as often as men do."*

Domestic Violence Against Men Is a Serious Problem

Tara Rempel

Tara Rempel wrote the following article for *Indian Life* magazine. In it, she asserts that female violence against men is a serious phenomenon that is often ignored in domestic violence studies. Rempel partly blames the dominance of feminist rhetoric for the lack of attention paid to husband and boyfriend abuse. She also notes that many male victims are too embarrassed by the social stigma of being beaten up by women to report such abuse. Rempel hopes that society will adopt "gender blindness" when dealing with all types of domestic abuse so that men who are abused will be taken seriously and be offered the help they need.

As you read, consider the following questions:

1. What does Rempel mean when she says that "violence against men is a common sight, even to the level of it being humorous"?
2. What two reasons does the author give to explain why male victims refrain from reporting their abuse?
3. Besides self-defense and retaliation, what is the third reason that women often strike out against men, according to Rempel?

Although for many it seems hard to believe, men in North American society are being domestically abused by their wives or girlfriends in roughly the same amount as women are abused by their male partners.

How often in a day do we North Americans see violence against men, both from other men and from women? Simply watching an hour or two of television will give some idea as to the answer. Violence against men is a common sight, even to the level of it being humorous. It is very common to see a woman strike a man in jest or in frustration or for whatever reason, more often than we would ever see a man strike a woman.

In fact, in our mainstream society the only time we see a man strike a woman, be it a slap, punch or push, is when a perpetrator or villain is abusing a woman. However, we often glimpse a woman slapping a man's face for something he said.

Defining Male Battery

Male battery is generally the same as domestic assault. Male battery is any violent behavior between adults in an intimate, sexual or cohabiting relationship. This includes: pushing, slapping, punching, kicking, breaking bones, cutting, killing, throwing objects, smashing items over the victim and choking, etc. Also considered domestic abuse would be some non-physical violence such as locking a person outside the house, leaving them in an unsafe area or destroying their belongings or pets.

Prevalence of Abuse

The statistics at this time show the numbers being roughly equal between men and women aggressors in the home. However, there is still some gender prejudice making those statistics a widely known fact.

Men's activists are on firmer ground when they point to a 1985 study, funded by the National Institute of Mental Health, that found women to be as physically abusive as men. But even those results must be interpreted with care. However, multiple other articles and researchers disagree with that statement saying the complete opposite that in terms of severe violence, the rate for women using severe forms of violence against men is almost twice as high as the rate of men using the same amount of severity on women. For example, "the rate of severe assaults by men on women in the home fell by almost 50 percent between the first National Family Violence Survey (1975) and the most recent update of data in 1992. It dropped from 38 per 1,000 couples per year to 20. But the rate of dangerous female assaults on males in the home stayed essentially static over that period—45 per 1,000 couples and is now twice as high as the male rate."

Feminist Issues

The truth is, women are just as violent as men and commit severe acts of violence against their partners almost twice as often as men do. In Los Angeles, for example, those rates have quadrupled [since 1993]. In Wisconsin, the rate of abusive men being referred from the courts to counseling has doubled since 1989, but the same referral of abusive women has multiplied twelve-fold in that time.

In the last 20 to 30 years, feminism has done a great deal to inform the public about the prevalence and terror of domestic abuse, however, until now, domestic abuse has only been something that can occur against women.

In the feminist perspective, men are thought of as aggressive, oppressors of women's rights and freedoms and domestic assault is one of the ways that those traits play out in our society. However, not everyone believes these things to be true.

Masculinity/Social Implications

For most men, the idea of being beaten up by a woman carries significant personal and social implications. The old mocking phrase "you hit like a girl" is still considered to be a serious insult to a boy, however, when a woman does physically harm her spouse, many men simply refuse to tell or seek help for because exactly those social and personal beliefs kick in.

For many men, having to admit that his wife has beaten or hurt him is to admit cowardice or weakness. ". . . men are reluctant to acknowledge that they have been beaten by their wives. The humiliation and embarrassment that accompanies all spouse abuse may be even greater for male victims,

**"If this marriage is going to work, you're going to
have to learn to control your temper."**

considering society's traditional values about male-female
relationships." Another reason men fear telling on their
wives is because they are afraid of losing their wife and family. There seems to be the belief in our society that men do
not care about their children as much as women do; however, that simply is not true. Many men interviewed in the
studies on male battery stated that the idea of losing their
children to their wives or to foster homes was a big reason
that they refused to report their wife's violence. "As an individual becomes more ashamed of an experience, he becomes
less likely to discuss it. This silence allows the violence to
persist, which can add to the man's embarrassment. The increased shame only furthers his need to remain silent?"

There are two general reasons why women strike out in

violence: 1) in self-defense; 2) retaliatory aggression.

However, this author would like to also note a third reason, simple violent nature and reasonless behavior.

The last area that needs to be addressed is that some women may be naturally more violent than other women or other men. When reviewing [professor Terrie] Moffitt's research, one author notes, "her research disputes a long-held belief about the nature of domestic violence: If a woman hits it's only in response to her partner's attacks. The study suggests that some women may simply be prone to violence—by nature or circumstance—just as some men may be."

In many cases, men alone perpetrate the violence in homes, and in many homes, approximately double the first situation, both the man and woman perpetrate the violence. However, in roughly the same amount of homes as the first situation, women alone perpetrate the violence. These are the homes where violence is committed against the male partner without instigation or retaliation.

Results of Male Battery

For all abuse victims, shame is the primary response to victimization. In abuse situations, a loss of personal power occurs, which creates fear, shame and especially for abused men, embarrassment. For women who are abused, embarrassment seems to be less significant socially since domestic abuse has become such a well-known problem. However, due to the socially and personally sensitive nature of domestic abuse against men, it is not as well known. In our society, when a woman is abused, the well-held beliefs of a man's superior strength and violent tendencies keep her from feeling like less of a woman. For men however, being beaten by a woman does, exactly that, it marginalizes his masculinity, or makes him feel as though, he is less of a man.

Our society needs to embrace the same notions of abuse and violence that it has towards women and echo them towards men. We need to embrace a notion of gender blindness when discussing domestic abuse, and stop assuming it cannot happen to men too. As this author sums up poignantly, "it is important to keep in mind that an abused husband is no less a victim because of his sex than an abused wife."

"Police, prosecutors and academics agree that women are still the ones who suffer the vast majority of injuries from domestic violence."

Domestic Violence Against Men Is Exaggerated

Christine Wicker

In the following viewpoint, Christine Wicker, a staff writer for the *Dallas Morning News*, argues that violence suffered by men in abusive relationships is not as severe as some men's advocates claim. Wicker does not deny that men can be victims of intimate violence, but because they are physically stronger than women, they are typically able to defend themselves and even inflict injury during any domestic squabble. Wicker notes that police and academics agree that women are still far more likely to be the victims and not the perpetrators of domestic violence.

As you read, consider the following questions:

1. Why is police detective R.D. Robinson hesitant to use the term *battered* to describe male victims of domestic abuse?
2. What are women batterers more likely guilty of, in the opinion of L. Kevin Hamberger?
3. How does Dallas County district attorney Cindy Dyer define "true battering"?

Jim says his former wife chased him around the yard with a butcher knife, threw plates of food in his direction and kicked him in the back one morning as he was shaving.

"I remember one night I was terrified. She was threatening to kill me and the kids. I didn't want to go to sleep," said the Dallas man, who asked that his real name not be used because he is afraid that his young son would be ridiculed.

He said he never hit his wife. "I tried to talk her down," said Jim. "I'm a social worker, and I never thought I was a victim of domestic violence. I never even put myself into the category of victim."

Jim's experience is far more common than most people believe, say men's rights activists. They say many men never mention intimate violence either because they aren't severely injured, don't think they'll be believed or are ashamed.

The advocates cite studies that show women, as often as men, hit, bite, scratch, shove or throw things at their intimate partners.

But police, prosecutors and academics agree that women are still the ones who suffer the vast majority of injuries from domestic violence.

And thereby hangs the controversy.

Murray Straus is the scholar most often cited by men's advocates on the subject. His 1975, 1985 and 1992 studies of American couples show females assaulting males 50 percent of the time—and often striking first.

His work has been widely criticized. But "it's not only my studies," said Dr. Straus, co-director of the Family Research Laboratory at the University of New Hampshire. "There are now more than a hundred studies that find the same thing.

"If you don't take into account the injury, if you don't take into account who feels dominated by whom" it's easy to believe that women are as menacing as men, said the sociology professor.

His work is used by people such as Arlington [Texas] father's rights advocate Roy Getting to say that battered men need shelters of their own. "Men are not making enough of what's happening to them," said Mr. Getting, who says battered men do exist and hopes to open a shelter for them in Arlington.

Dr. Straus disagrees. "We don't need shelters for men," he

said. They aren't being physically injured in the way women are, partly because women aren't strong enough and partly, he says, because women aren't as willing to hurt men.

Men who experience continual acts of violence by women "are serious victims in that that's a hell of a life to lead," he said.

Men's advocates say widespread violence against men goes unnoticed by police and emergency room doctors who are trained to look for domestic abuse against women only.

"I have not seen it," said Mesquite [Texas] police detective R.D. Robinson. As many as 90 domestic assault complaints pass over his desk in a month, many filed by men, he said. But he wouldn't call those men battered. "The assault occurred but not a serious bodily assault," he said.

In a 1994 study of emergency room admissions sponsored by the U.S. Department of Justice, 37 percent of women reported being injured by their domestic partners compared to 4.5 percent of men. Some of those were gay people injured by same-sex partners.

"One of the worst cases of battered women syndrome I've ever seen was a man battered by another man," said Dallas County District Attorney Cindy Dyer.

Steve Storie, an investigator with the Dallas district attorney's family violence unit, said that if domestic violence against men were a big problem, "we'd have a men's shelter on every corner with a golf course and valet parking.

"I'll handle every case in the State of Texas of women who batter men on a continual basis. Just give them all to me, and I'll have plenty of time," said Mr. Storie, who was a police officer for 22 years.

"I can tell you this," he added. "I don't sit here fainting and crying over pictures of what women have done to men. It's the other way around."

Hardly anyone denies that men are sometimes serious victims of female violence. "Some of the most aggressive people I've seen in policing are females in bar fights," said Dallas police Sgt. C.I. Williams, who heads the Dallas family violence unit. "It's naive to think that doesn't happen in domestic situations."

On the other hand, he said, "When you look at crime

statistics in general, men commit the vast majority of assaults, and there's no reason to think that's not true in families, too."

The picture is complicated by the issue of male pride.

"First the man has to admit to himself and then admit to an outsider that he's been assaulted and that's pretty tough for a man's ego to handle," said Mr. Getting.

Police say many men are quite willing to say that their wives and girlfriends hit them, but that their stories don't hold up.

"If Mary scratches you on the arm and you break her nose and blacken both her eyes, you're going to be guilty of assault," said Sgt. Williams.

A Crime Too Rare

"Men are sometimes victims of domestic violence," said Nancy Scannell, legislative director of Jane Doe Inc., a Massachusetts-based domestic violence coalition. "But the attempt to be inclusive [of male victims] should never be interpreted to mean that the issue is gender-neutral. . . ."

Katherine Greene, Jane Doe's public affairs director, said cases of battered men—true victims of one-sided abuse—are too rare to warrant a massive change in the domestic violence agenda.

"Sometimes it snows in Florida," she said, quoting a Jane Doe board member's comment on male victims at an annual board meeting. "We can't ignore it, but we don't make public policy around it."

Farah Stockman, "A Search for Equality, Domestic Abuse Groups Dispute Status of Claims Made by Men," *Boston Globe*, October 28, 2002.

Men's advocates say an increasing number of women are assaulting men as a way of luring them into violence.

"One thing that happens a lot is that women's divorce attorneys tell them that one way to assure you get custody is to provoke your partner to slap you or kick or assault you in some way. You file a protective order and there's no way he will get the kids," said therapist Stephen Finstein, mental health adviser for Fathers for Equal Rights.

Pat Keene, a lawyer who often deals with women seeking protective orders, calls that idea ludicrous.

"I would never never advise someone to provoke violence.

It puts their lives in jeopardy. Once the violence starts you can't be sure the perpetrator won't turn around and hurt one of the children as well," she said.

The point that fathers' advocates want to make is that violence is a two-way street, said Ned Holstein, a physician who is president of Fathers and Families in Boston.

"Men living in fear and being controlled by violence is not much of a problem," he said. "What is a problem is thousands of children having their fathers taken away because of an exaggerated and one-sided portrayal of domestic violence as being something only men do."

On the other side, many experts say women most often lash out in self-defense or retaliation for previous assaults.

When Dr. Robert Muelleman studied victims of domestic violence in an inner-city public hospital in Kansas City, he found that half the men who reported being injured by women had previous convictions for domestic violence.

L. Kevin Hamberger found that women who use violence against their partners are acting in self-defense or retaliation two-thirds of the time.

"Even some of the women who say, 'I use violence to control my partner,' are battered women . . . who decided, 'I'm not taking this. I'm paying him back,'" said Dr. Hamberger, professor of family and community medicine at the Medical College of Wisconsin in Milwaukee.

Police, shelter workers, emergency room doctors and family violence prosecutors agree with men's rights advocates that there are nonviolent men being physically injured by female partners.

When men's groups put out requests for Dallas-area battered men to come forward, numerous men responded.

Some said they were being emotionally, financially and legally abused but not beaten. Others called to say they knew men physically abused by women in dramatic and dangerous ways, but they could not supply details.

Half a dozen men told stories of various physical assaults.

"Would you call drawing blood abuse?" asked one man, who didn't give his name. His wife awakens him three or four times a week by digging her fingernails into him, he said.

Another man, who didn't want his name used, said his

wife attacked him in the groin area. Both he and his former wife had filed for protective orders. She got hers. He didn't. Anti-male prejudice was to blame, he said.

Mr. Finstein located three men who he said were strong examples of abuse. But as he predicted, the men downplayed the idea that they were victims. One told of his wife pushing and shoving but said physical violence wasn't a big factor in the relationship.

"It was just dirty down, cruddy living," he said of life with his former wife.

Another man had multiple arrests for domestic violence. His wife hit him and otherwise provoked him into hitting her, he said.

"We both fought," he said, admitting that he bloodied her mouth and blacked her eyes. "To me it seemed like she was the one who started it. . . . Physically she would get the worst of it, but then I would be the one sitting in jail."

A former drug abuser said his wife became physically violent when he started cleaning up his own life. "Abusers use guilt and shame to control you. Once they lose those weapons, it escalates. That's what happened to me," he said.

Dr. Muelleman thinks some of the violence among American couples is what he calls "mutual combat."

"He's no more an abuser than she is. At least, that's what the women tell me. They say, 'We just fight.' I'll ask, 'Do you feel controlled?' and she'll say, 'No.'"

True battering is about controlling another person's life, said Ms. Dyer, who heads a unit specifically devoted to domestic violence. Few men are being battered in that way and many women are, she said.

"There are many controlling women but they don't typically use force," she said. "They use emotional tools rather than physical threats."

Dr. Straus agrees that women don't often manage to dominate men through violence but does believe they use violence to gain control. He also believes "violence by women is a serious social problem that cannot be ignored."

The so-called harmless kicks and slaps women deliver "keep women at risk," said the professor.

"He's a slob. So she hits him and when she does, she establishes the principle that it's morally right to hit when someone does something you don't like. . . . The problem with that is that sooner or later it's going to be her turn to do something that he doesn't like. That's the nature of marriage, and she has unwittingly provided the justification for him hitting her," he said.

"The principle has to be that there's no hitting by anyone in this family."

"Domestic violence between same-sex partners is a subject that has been largely avoided by governments, law enforcement, and society."

Domestic Violence Is a Serious Problem for Homosexuals

Linda M. Peterman and Charlotte G. Dixon

In the following viewpoint, Linda M. Peterman and Charlotte G. Dixon assert that domestic violence is a serious concern in the gay community. The authors maintain, however, that awareness is lacking for several reasons. First, abused homosexuals are apt to keep quiet and refrain from reporting intimate violence. Second, there are few services designed to aid homosexual victims of domestic abuse. Finally, gay men and lesbians exhibit the same types of partner loyalty, financial dependence, fear, and other emotional connectedness that keeps abused heterosexual spouses in their troubled relationships. Peterman and Dixon urge homosexuals and society to end the denial and bring this problem to light. Linda M. Peterman is a member of Global Therapy, a mental health facility in Tampa, Florida. Charlotte G. Dixon is with the Department of Rehabilitation and Mental Health Counseling at the University of South Florida.

As you read, consider the following questions:

1. According to the authors, what are the only other health problems in the gay community that are more widespread than domestic violence?
2. As cited by Peterman and Dixon, what reasons do homosexuals give for staying in abusive relationships?

Linda M. Peterman and Charlotte G. Dixon, "Domestic Violence Between Same-Sex Partners: Implications for Counseling," *Journal of Counseling and Development*, Winter 2003. Copyright © 2003 by the *Journal of Counseling and Development*. Reproduced by permission.

Over the past 2 decades, awareness and concern about the incidence and severity of domestic violence have increased. Although information about domestic violence has grown, much of the literature does not address domestic violence between same-sex partners. This article discusses the dynamics of domestic violence between partners of the same sex. The social and cultural issues in the gay and lesbian communities play a large part in perpetuating the myths of domestic violence, which keeps the abuse hidden. This article is based on an extensive review of the literature and a clinical consensus among experts in the field.

Domestic violence is a major social and health problem in the United States that affects the family, society, and the future. Between 2 and 4 million women in the U.S. are physically battered annually by their partners, and 25% to 30% of all U.S. women are at risk of domestic violence during their lifetime. In 1992, the U.S. Surgeon General declared domestic violence this nation's number one health problem. Domestic violence is also prevalent in the gay and lesbian communities, occurring with the same or even greater frequency than in heterosexual communities. The National Coalition Against Domestic Violence estimates that 25% to 33% of all same-sex relationships include domestic violence.

The Rates of Violence

Domestic violence is the third largest health problem facing gay men today, second to substance abuse and AIDS. In heterosexual couples, it is estimated that the man is the abuser in 95% of the cases. [D.] Island and [P.] Letellier reported [in 1991] that gay men's domestic violence might occur at a rate greater than heterosexual violence because both partners in a homosexual relationship are men and each has the same probability of being an abuser. In addition, gay men are not less violent than straight men. According to W.O.M.E.N. Inc., a San Francisco organization serving battered women, domestic violence also occurs in one of four lesbian relationships. For example, 50% of lesbians polled at the 1985 Michigan women's music festival said that they had been a victim of domestic violence by a female partner. Fifty percent of those surveyed also said they had been the abuser in a same-sex relationship. Lesbians have worked in domestic violence shelters as counselors and volunteers and have played an active role in the battered women's movement since it began. They have fought against men's violent behavior against women. However, some researchers suggested that the lesbian community chooses to believe that women are not abusive or violent. The idea of a lesbian being an abuser is considered impossible, and therefore domestic violence is largely ignored or kept quiet in the lesbian community.

Keeping It Quiet

Besides being ignored in the gay and lesbian communities themselves, domestic violence between same-sex partners is a subject that has been largely avoided by governments, law enforcement, and society. Gay men and lesbians are less likely to report the abuse and more likely to stay with their partner because of homophobia, heterosexism [a belief that it is more normal in society to be heterosexual], and ignorance in the community regarding domestic violence as well as homosexuality. Furthermore, some gay men and lesbians have internalized society's prejudices against them and believe they deserve to be violated.

Although books and magazine articles regarding same-sex domestic violence issues started appearing in the late 1980s, adequate support groups, shelters, and treatment programs for this population are still not in place. For example, as of 1997, no shelters existed for gay men, although in some cities battered men can obtain hotel vouchers from domestic violence centers. [S.] Friess [1997] indicated that many support groups would not allow gay men to attend because some people believe it creates a volatile situation among men already prone to violence. [T.] Akpodiete (1993) and [K.] Lobel (1986) further suggested that even when lesbians go to domestic violence shelters, they are discriminated against just because the word lesbian produces fear in others. Depending on the degree of homophobia present within an agency, services, intake procedures, forms, and personnel in abuse shelters may be discriminatory toward gay men and lesbians. . . .

[C.M.] Renzetti (1992) conducted a groundbreaking nationwide study on lesbian battering using 100 female participants who identified themselves as victims of lesbian battering. According to Renzetti, there are three types of abusive lesbian relationships: situational battering, chronic battering, and emotional or psychological battering. Situational battering occurs once or twice as a result of some situational event and is the least common. Chronic battering is when physical abuse has occurred more than two times and escalates over time. The emotional battering relationship is one in which the abuse is verbal or psychological rather than physical. Many times a relationship consists of physical and psychological battering. In Renzetti's study, 87% of the women reported both physical and psychological abuse; however, psychological abuse was more frequent. Most forms of physical and psychological abuse in lesbian relationships are similar to those in heterosexual relationships. Table 1 summarizes some common abusive behaviors. However, in same-sex relationships, abusers may also threaten to expose their partner's sexual preference to their friends, family, community, church, or employer. This is even more of a problem for bisexuals, who run the risk of being unwillingly exposed to both the heterosexual and the homosexual communities. . . .

Batterers and Their Victims

Domestic violence is not about strength; it is a pattern of behaviors designed to control another. Consequently, women as well as men are capable of physical, sexual, emotional, verbal, and economic abuse and other controlling behaviors. There is no profile of a "typical" batterer. In other words, all batterers will not exhibit the same behavior or the same thought patterns. However, they usually believe the following: They are entitled to control their partner, violence is permissible, violence will produce the desired effect, violence will not unduly endanger them. Batterers want or need to have power and control over their partner; therefore, they will resort to intimidation, threats, coercion, and violence to obtain this power. . . .

Like the abusers, victims who are battered come from all walks of life. Although there is no psychological profile of those who will be battered, there are common characteristics of victims once they have been abused. All victims of do-

Table 1: Types of Abuse and Behaviors

Type of Abuse	Behaviors
Physical abuse	Punching, shoving, slapping, biting, kicking, using a weapon against partner, throwing items, breaking items, pulling hair, restraining partner
Emotional/verbal abuse	Putting partner down, calling names, criticizing, playing mind games, humiliating partner, making partner feel guilty, reinforcing internalized homophobia
Financial dependency	Keeping partner from getting a job, getting partner fired from job, making partner ask for money or taking partner's money, expecting partner to support them
Social isolation	Controlling who partner sees and talks to and where partner goes, limiting partner's involvement in gay and lesbian community
Sexual abuse	Forcing partner to perform sexual acts that are uncomfortable to him or her, engaging in affairs, telling partner he or she asked for the abuse (in S&M relationship), telling partner what to wear, accusing partner of affairs, criticizing sexual performance, withholding affection
Minimizing/denying	Making light of abuse, saying abuse did not happen, saying the abuse was mutual, blaming partner for abuse
Coercion/threats/ intimidation	Making partner afraid by looks or gestures; destroying property; hurting pets; displaying weapons; threatening to leave, take children, or commit suicide; threatening to reveal homosexuality to community, employer, family, or ex-spouse

mestic violence experience shame, embarrassment, isolation, and repressed feelings. [J.] Neisen (1993) wrote that similar traits are seen in those suffering from heterosexism and in victims of domestic violence. Therefore, gay and lesbian victims of domestic violence may be suffering from victimization by society as well as their partner. . . .

Remaining in an Abusive Relationship

Both abusers and their partners can be extremely dependent on each other as a result of negative self-images. Renzetti's study showed that when an abusive lesbian becomes more dependent on the victim and the victim becomes more autonomous, the abuse increases. The fear of more abuse keeps victims isolated and prevents them from telling anyone about the abuse they have endured. Also, many persons who are gay or lesbian do not want anyone to know of the abuse for they fear society thinking that the homosexual community is "sick," "violent," or "uncontrollable."

Therefore, gay women usually only receive emotional support from the lesbian community. Because many lesbian couples share close friends, a victim may be in a dilemma regarding the choice or availability of those she is able to confide in. She must choose between embarrassing and alienating her partner and the risk of abandonment by her friends if they take her partner's side. Also, after a battering incident, the batterer frequently is the sole source of support and comfort for the victim due to isolation. . . .

Other reasons named by lesbians and gay men that keep them in an abusive relationship are similar to those that heterosexual women give for staying in such a situation. Victims stay with their abusive partners because of fear, love, hope, pride, embarrassment, loyalty, financial dependence, low self-esteem, religious beliefs, children, and ignorance. In Renzetti's study of lesbian victims, love is the primary reason they stay in the relationship, combined with the hope that their partner will change. In addition, homosexual victims do not want their partners arrested for the same reasons given by heterosexual victims. The arrest can lead to embarrassment, financial loss, retaliation, and homophobic abusive treatment by the police, the judicial system, and the press. . . .

The Myth of Mutual Battering

It is a myth that same-sex domestic violence is associated with mutual battering or mutual abuse. Mutual battering is the idea that each partner is both a perpetrator and a victim of abuse. This concept actually minimizes the violence in same-sex relationships. One major difference between women who are battered by women and women who are battered by men is that lesbian women report fighting back more often. However, there are differences among using violence in self-defense, retaliating against a violent partner, and initiating violence. Lobel wrote that lesbians might fight back more because self-defense courses are more widespread in the feminist/lesbian community. In addition to self-defense, fighting back is usually a result of built-up rage from past abuse. The person who is the abuser in a same-sex relationship may be the physically stronger one; however, if he or she is the weaker one, he or she uses other tactics to control, intimidate, and coerce his or her partner. Also, same-sex partners can more easily fight back because their physical size tends to be closer to that of their partners' size. However, when victims fight back, they usually feel guilty for their own behavior or are told they are also abusive. Such feedback may prevent them from seeking help or reporting future incidents of abuse.

Violent Incidents Among Older Homosexuals

The incidence of abuse among the elder population is on the rise. According to the Administration on Aging (2000) fact sheet, hundreds of thousands of older persons are abused, neglected, and exploited by family members and others each year. Due to underreporting of abuse, the exact incidence of elder abuse is unknown; however, reports of domestic elder abuse to adult protective services increased 150% between 1986 and 1996. As the general population of older Americans continues to grow, it is estimated that the prevalence of elder abuse will also continue to increase.

Issues of abuse among the older population of gay men and lesbians have gained attention in the recent past. In fact, the featured theme of a 1999 conference sponsored by Senior Action in Gay Environment was elder abuse among those in the gay community. There are several factors that may contribute to the growth of domestic violence among older gay men and lesbians. First, in order to survive in a homophobic society, many older gay men and lesbians have become very independent, contributing to increased isolation and vulnerability in old age. Second, many gay men and lesbians may believe it is too risky to open their personal lives up to a society that has been hostile and judgmental in the past. As a result, they fear reaching out for help from domestic violence centers, law enforcement, or court personnel. Third, many who have been in long-term, same-sex relationships may have assets tied up in joint accounts, such as homes, retirement funds, savings, and so on. Should one partner desire to leave the relationship, there may be limited and questionable legal recourse available in most states resulting in a situation that could have a significant negative impact on one's financial stability in old age. To avoid a potentially difficult and costly legal case, as well as the threat of financial instability, the older homosexual may remain in an abusive relationship. Fourth, older homosexuals also may be at a greater risk for becoming or remaining victims of domestic violence due to the fear that because of their age and their isolation, they may be unable to find other partners. . . .

End the Denial

Despite the similarities, a number of differences compound the severity of domestic violence experienced by gay men and lesbians. Any person, male or female or gay or straight, has the potential to be an abuser. Regardless of whether or not the abuse is among heterosexual or same-sex partners, society has always been hesitant to intervene in domestic violence. Society and the gay and lesbian communities must put an end to denial of abuse in same-sex relationships. Society's denial and the victims' silence due to shame, isolation, embarrassment, and fear have prevented victims from leaving abusive relationships and perpetrators from receiving help. In addition, society's ignorance of the needs of gay men and lesbian women, as proven by the lack of services available to help them, allows the abuse to continue. With acceptance, awareness, and education, domestic violence can be suppressed in all of society's populations.

> *"As women's alternatives to their relationships improve, they should experience less violence."*

Domestic Violence Is Decreasing

Amy Farmer and Jill Tiefenthaler

According to a Department of Justice press release in the year 2000, incidents of reported domestic violence against women decreased 20 percent from 1993 through 1998. In the following article, Amy Farmer and Jill Tiefenthaler account for the overall decline. They explain that the availability of social and legal services has provided abused women an outlet to remedy their problems. The authors also contend that the growing economic power of women has given them the independence to leave abusive relationships. Amy Farmer is an associate professor of economics at the University of Arkansas. Jill Tiefenthaler is an associate professor of economics at Colgate University in New York. Their work on this project was completed while they were fellows at the Carnegie Mellon Census Research Data Center.

As you read, consider the following questions:

1. According to the Department of Justice press release, as cited by Farmer and Tiefenthaler, what percentage of women nationwide had a college degree in 1998?
2. According to the authors, the most likely female victims of abuse are between what ages?
3. As Farmer and Tiefenthaler report, what happens to the level of domestic abuse when welfare payments rise?

Amy Farmer and Jill Tiefenthaler, "Explaining the Recent Decline in Domestic Violence," *Contemporary Economic Policy*, April 2003. Copyright © 2003 by Oxford University Press. Reproduced by permission of the publisher and the authors.

In a recent press release (May 17, 2000), the DOJ [Department of Justice] Bureau of Justice Statistics (BJS) reports that violence against women by intimate partners fell by 21% from 1993 through 1998. This statistic was calculated from the NCVS [National Crime Victimization Survey], an annual survey on the incidence of all types of crimes, including violence by intimates (current or former spouses, girlfriends, or boyfriends). National estimates on the rate of domestic violence are only available from 1993 because the NCVS (formerly called the National Crime Survey [NCS]) was significantly redesigned in 1992. Previous estimates of intimate partner abuse were found to suffer from a serious problem of underreporting, but the redesigned survey includes several questions specifically concerning intimate partner abuse. However, trend data are available on intimate partner homicide since the 1970s, and these data support a long-term decline in domestic violence. The BJS reports that between 1976 and 1998, the number of male victims of intimate partner homicide fell an average 4% per year, and the number of female victims fell an average 1% per year.

In addition to documenting the decline in the rate of domestic abuse, the BJS report by [C.M.] Rennison and [S.] Welchans (2000) outlines the characteristics of the victims. Data from the NCVS indicate that being young, black, poor, and divorced or separated all increase the likelihood of a woman being a victim of intimate partner abuse. Specifically, women ages 20–24 are the most likely to be victimized, and black women are 35% more likely to be abused than white women and 2.5 times more likely than women of other races. Women in the lowest income households have seven times the abuse rates of those in the highest income households. Finally, women with children under age 12 experience twice the rate of abuse than those without young children.

What factors explain the apparent decline in intimate partner abuse? Economic theory predicts that the incidence of abuse declines as women gain economic independence and therefore gain power in their relationships. Farmer and Tiefenthaler (1997) show that as women's alternatives to their relationships improve, they should experience less violence because as women gain credible threats to exit their relationships, they can assert more power within the relationships. Men are forced to lessen the violence or risk losing their partners. Consequently, women are more likely to leave, or they suffer less violence if they choose to stay. Given this theory, the authors expect that as women's outside alternatives improve, intimate partner abuse should decline. This could occur due to improvements in individual women's economic status. Women who have greater earnings or earning potential are more likely to leave abusive relationships because they can support themselves. If men respond to women's increased power by lowering the violence, women may decide to stay, but clearly the incidence of violence has declined and the women are better off. In addition, overall gender equality in the community might provide battered women with better alternatives and therefore more credible threats of leaving. For example, a woman's threat to leave her abuser is much more credible if she lives in an area where a large percentage of women are employed and women's wages are high. Finally, outside options could also be improved via services provided to help battered women, such as shelters, welfare benefits, and civil legal services to assist women with protection orders, child support, and custody.

Better Alternatives

Farmer and Tiefenthaler (1997) find support for the theory as women who with the highest personal incomes (this includes both wages and nonwage income, such as child support and public assistance) experience the least amount of abuse. The BJS finding that poor, young, minority women with young children are most likely to be victims of intimate partner abuse is also consistent with the theory given that these women have the fewest alternatives to their relationships. Other studies support the notion that women's alternatives affect the level of violence that they experience. [R.J.] Gelles (1976) and [M.D.] Pagelow (1981) both find evidence that women with access to fewer resources are less likely to leave their abusers. [D.] Kalmuss and [M.] Straus (1990) indicate that women who are highly dependent on marriage suffer greater abuse, whereas several studies find that women in male-dominated marriages experience more violence. Finally, overall gender inequality has been linked to higher rates of abuse across states and countries.

Although the empirical literature supports the importance of women's economic alternatives as a determinant of domestic violence, there is little empirical work that examines the effect of service provision on the rate of female abuse. However, one study does examine the effect of service provision on the rate at which women kill their husbands. [L.] Dugan et al. (1998) examines the effects of domesticity, women's economic power, and resources for battered women on intimate partner homicides in 29 U.S. cities over four biannual periods. The results indicate that both women's economic power and services provided for battered women lower the rate at which women kill their husbands. The authors contend that women with better alternatives are more likely to use them rather than resort to killing their abusers to protect themselves. . . .

Services, Education, and Income

The expansion of legal assistance to battered women has accounted for part of the decline in the incidence of domestic violence nationwide. The expansion of legal services has mostly resulted from existing programs for victims of intimate partner abuse adding legal services to their lists of services provided as opposed to new programs opening their doors. Part of the credit for the expansion of legal services goes to the federal government. With the passage of the Violence against Women Act in 1994, the federal government made a commitment to meet the needs of women who are victims of violence. . . .

Another important determinant of the likelihood of a woman reporting abuse is education. Both the woman's own educational status (having a college degree) and the relative education of women in her community (the percent of women in the county with college degrees relative to the percent of men in the county with college degrees) significantly impact the likelihood of abuse. From 1993 to 1998, the percentage of women nationwide with college degrees increased from 17.9% to 20.7%, an increase of almost 16%. The increase was even more significant for black women increasing from 10.9% to 13.6%, representing more than a 35% increase in the proportion of college-educated black women. The increase in women's educational attainment over the time period is likely to play a substantial role in diminishing the incidence of domestic abuse.

Rate of Violence by an Intimate Partner, by Gender, 1993–1998

Number of victimizations by an intimate partner
per 1,000 persons of each gender age 12 or older

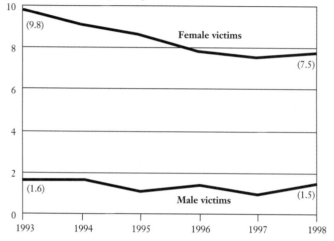

Callie Marie Rennison and Sarah Welchans, "Intimate Partner Violence,"
Bureau of Justice Statistics Special Report, May 2000.

Household income is also found to be a significant predictor of the likelihood that the woman is a victim of domestic violence. Household income is likely to be significant both because women are more likely to have earnings, and therefore economic power, in households with higher incomes and because as men's incomes (and education status) increase, they are less likely to abuse their partners. The suggestion that women's economic power is at least partially the explanation for the negative relationship between household income and domestic violence is supported by the fact that when household income is dropped from the list of independent variables, women's employment status has a significant and negative effect on the likelihood of abuse.

According to census statistics, over the period from 1993 to 1998, both median household income and women's median income increased. Median household income in 1993 (1998 adjusted dollars) was $35,241. By 1998 that figure has risen to $38,885, an increase of 10.3%. The economic prosperity of the 1990s has been cited as a likely cause of the decrease in the overall crime rate, and it appears to have been a cause of the decrease in domestic violence as well. Women's median income increased almost 18% from $13,800 to $16,258 (1998 adjusted dollars). Not only did women's real income rise, indicating an increase in outside options, but women's income as a percentage of men's income rose over this period as well. In 1993 women's median income was 49.7% of men's, whereas in 1998 that figure had increased to 53.0%. An increase in women's earning power relative to men's implies that women have both more opportunities for self-sufficiency and fewer gains from marriage. Both of these factors will increase the likelihood that women leave abusive relationships. Finally, women's labor force participation rate rose two percentage points from 58.5% in 1993 to 60.5% in 1998.

Age, Race, and Children

One of the most important demographic trends of the twenty-first century will be the increasing age of the populations in developed countries. This demographic trend, which started in the late twentieth century, appears to have an important impact on the incidence of domestic violence. Younger women experience significantly more violence with women between the ages of 20 and 24 most likely to be victims. During the 1990s, the percentage of women in this age category fell from 35.8% in 1993 to 32.0% in 1998. This decline of 3.8 percentage points represents a 10.6% decline in the percentage of the U.S. population that belongs to the highest risk age group. As the population continues to age, the incidence of domestic violence will continue to decline.

Race is also a significant factor in the reported incidence of abuse and the changing racial composition of the current population, another important demographic trend that will continue in the twenty-first century, appears to be another significant factor in explaining the decline in domestic violence. Although the BJS report suggests that black women are more likely to be abuse victims, once other factors such as income and marital status are controlled for, this study finds that black women are less likely to be abused than their non-Hispanic white counterparts. Similarly, we find that Hispanic women as well as women of all other races are less likely to be victims than non-Hispanic white women. The percentage of the female population that is white non-Hispanic fell 1.2 percentage points, from 38.1% to 36.9%, between 1993 and 1998. This decline represents a significant demographic shift over such a short period of time. Holding other factors constant, as the population continues to become more racially diverse, the reported incidence of domestic violence should continue to decline. However, if the increase in racial diversity is the result of increased immigration and therefore is accompanied by lower educational status among women (and men) and more poor households, one is not likely to see a decline in intimate partner abuse.

The number of children that a woman has is also a significant determinant of abuse. Women with children, especially young children, are more dependent on their relationships and have fewer alternatives for self-sufficiency outside their relationships and consequently are more likely to be abused. Although the fertility rate declined dramatically in previous decades, there was no significant change in this variable in the 1990s, and therefore it is not a significant factor in explaining the decline in domestic violence.

Marriage, Location, and Welfare

The regression results indicate that married women are less likely to report being abused. During the period from 1993 to 1998, the percentage of married women fell from 56.5% to 54.9%, representing a 1.6 percentage point drop. As a result, the authors expect that the increase in the percentages of divorced and separated women would increase the rate of reported intimate partner abuse. Clearly, any positive effect of the increase in divorce on domestic violence is outweighed by trends in other more important variables.

In addition to individual characteristics, this article finds that some community variables matter as well. Geographic location, possibly indicative of cultural norms and attitudes, is a significant predictor of the likelihood of abuse. Specifically, women living in the East North Central, East South Central, West South Central, Mountain, and Pacific regions report more abuse than women living in New England, the Middle and South Atlantic, and the West North Central regions of the country. The states with the greatest population increases in the 1990s are in the Pacific, Mountain, and South Atlantic regions. Although women living in the Pacific and Mountain regions experience significantly more violence, those living in the South Atlantic do not. However, given the magnitude of the population increases in the Pacific and Mountain regions relative to the rest of the United States (8 of 10 states with the greatest population growth are in these two regions), this variable does not generally support the trend to lower rates of abuse and may in fact be working in the opposite direction.

Finally, the authors find that as welfare payments rise, so does abuse. Given that the 1996 welfare reform has decreased the overall generosity of most states' welfare programs, this result is consistent with a lower national rate of abuse. However, the positive relationship between abuse and welfare generosity is a curious result with no theoretical basis. It may be explained by women leaving abusive relationships migrate to states that offer more generous support. In any case, one should be very careful in citing decreased welfare generosity as a source of the national decline in domestic violence.

This analysis indicates that more widespread provision of legal services for battered women, improved educational and economic status for women, and demographic trends explain the decline in domestic violence in the 1990s. With the exception of migration to the Mountain and Pacific regions of the country, a slight decline in marriage rates, and the fact that the average number of children has remained constant in the 1990s, every significant variable in our regression is trending in a direction that predicts a lower rate of abuse. . . .

As previously discussed, the incidence of domestic violence declined by 21% between 1993 and 1998 from 1.1 million violent incidents to 876,340 incidents. Therefore, the probability of an individual woman being abused fell from 0.011% to 0.0084% a decline in the likelihood of being abused of 0.0026%. . . . These results suggest that past trends that are likely to continue into the twenty-first century will have a significant impact on the incidence of domestic violence in the United States in the future.

Periodical Bibliography

The following articles have been selected to supplement the diverse views presented in this chapter.

Deborah J. Anderson   "The Impact of Subsequent Violence of Returning to an Abusive Partner," *Journal of Comparative Family Studies*, Winter 2003.

Tisha Gangopadhyay Armstrong et al.   "Disagreement About the Occurrence of Male-to-Female Intimate Partner Violence: A Qualitative Study," *Family and Community Health*, April 2001.

B.M. Barnes   "Family Violence Knows No Cultural Boundaries," *Journal of Family and Consumer Sciences*, November 1, 2001.

H.N. Bui and M. Morash   "Domestic Violence in the Vietnamese Immigrant Community: An Exploratory Study," *Violence Against Women*, July 1999.

J. Michael Cruz   "Why Doesn't He Just Leave?: Gay Male Domestic Violence and the Reasons Victims Stay," *Journal of Men's Studies*, Spring 2003.

Richard B. Felson et al.   "Reasons for Reporting and Not Reporting Domestic Violence to the Police," *Criminology*, August 2002.

Jana L. Jasinski   "Physical Violence Among Anglo, African American, and Hispanic Couples: Ethnic Differences in Persistence and Cessation," *Violence and Victims*, October 2001.

Holly Johnson   "The Cessation of Assaults on Wives," *Journal of Comparative Family Studies*, Winter 2003.

Jordan I. Kosberg   "The Abuse of Elderly Men," *Journal of Elder Abuse & Neglect*, vol. 9, 1998.

Dorothy Lemmey et al.   "Severity of Violence Against Women Correlates with Behavioral Problems in Their Children," *Pediatric Nursing*, May 2001.

Suzanne G. Martin   "Children Exposed to Domestic Violence: Psychological Considerations for Health Care Practitioners," *Holistic Nursing Practice*, April 2002.

Glenn Sacks   "Domestic Violence: A Two-Way Street," *Los Angeles Daily Journal*, October 15, 2001.

Cathy Young   "Oh Dad, Poor Dad: In Abuse, Men Are Victims, Too," *Boston Globe*, June 16, 2003.

CHAPTER 2

What Causes
Domestic Violence?

Chapter Preface

According to social learning theory, violence toward others is a learned behavior. Using this hypothesis, Steven Swinford and colleagues followed the progress of several hundred children and teenagers (ages twelve to nineteen) in Toledo, Ohio, over a ten-year period (1982–1992). At the end of the study, the boys and girls, now young adults, were questioned about the harshness of discipline they received from their parents while growing up. The interviewees were asked, for example, if they had been "spanked with a belt or strap," "hit with an object such as a stick," "hit with a closed fist," or "thrown against a wall." The subjects were then asked if they had engaged in or experienced any violence in their own relationships in the past year.

The results of this study were published in 2000. Swinford and colleagues found that those children who had received the severest physical discipline as children were more likely to perpetrate violence in intimate adult relationships. Therefore, the study contended that harsh physical punishment received as a child was a significant predictor of later domestic violence. In light of social learning theory, the researchers did not conclude that experiencing abusive punishment as children meant that the young men and women in the study felt the need to take out their own anger from past victimization on their current partners. Rather, experiencing parental abuse taught the children that violence was acceptable in close relationships. The study also found that the correlation between harsh discipline and later violence was not affected by race. Furthermore, the women in the study were noted to be more prone to perpetrating later violence yet less likely to have been victimized by it as children.

The "harsh discipline" study is somewhat atypical in that it looks to childhood experience for influences upon adult domestic violence. Most research into the causes of domestic violence focuses on the environment, psychology, and vices of perpetrators as adults. Income level, substance abuse, male power, and social norms are among the more common contributing factors debated in domestic violence studies. The impact of each of these potential causes of domestic violence, however, is still hotly contested, as the viewpoints in the following chapter illustrate. Yet whether examining childhood trauma or adult drug use, researchers continue to unravel the roots of domestic violence in the hope that determining its causes will lead to effective treatment to curb the problem.

"Our social structures themselves often reflect inequitable gender relationships that serve to maintain the legitimacy of male violence."

Patriarchy Causes Domestic Violence

Amy J. Marin and Nancy Felipe Russo

In the following viewpoint, Amy J. Marin and Nancy Felipe Russo contend that domestic violence is not attributable to psychological or biological urges in men (as other theoretical models suggest) but to a socially conditioned belief that women should always be the subordinate sex. The general lack of legal, political, and law enforcement concern for the problem reflects the fact that these institutions are also designed to maintain the patriarchal order in society. Marin and Russo assert that feminist theory has done much to explain the deeper motives behind violence against women and has transformed the problem from a private affair to a public concern. Amy J. Marin is a professor of psychology at Phoenix College. Nancy Felipe Russo is a regents professor of psychology at Arizona State University. She is also a former member of the American Psychological Association Task Force on Male Violence Against Women.

As you read, consider the following questions:

1. According to the authors, how are the terms *marital violence* and *domestic violence* politicized?
2. In what ways do the legal and judicial systems perpetuate partner violence, according to Marin and Russo?

Amy J. Marin and Nancy Felipe Russo, "Feminist Perspectives on Male Violence Against Women," *What Causes Men's Violence Against Women?* edited by Michèle Harway and James M. O'Neil. Thousand Oaks, CA: Sage Publications, 1999. Copyright © 1999 by Sage Publications, Inc. Reproduced by permission.

Feminists have done more than simply bring attention to the problems of male violence against women. Feminists have made such violence a central issue in the women's movement around the world. They have organized shelters, developed public education programs, advocated new laws and policies, promoted change in the criminal justice and health care systems, and fostered the development of a new knowledge base that reflects the realities of diverse women's lives.

Feminist writing and theorizing have qualitatively changed the way that researchers and scientists conceptualize and study the many forms of male violence against women. In the 1970s, rape was a central feminist issue. Academicians during this period of time also were becoming concerned with the issues of rape and domestic violence. However, researchers generally limited their investigations to studies of either the psychological characteristics of the individual perpetrator and/or victim, or an investigation of family relationships. They did not emphasize gender, power, or structural dimensions of violence. Feminist writers, in contrast, emphasized such issues and began to reconstruct rape and other forms of male violence as forms of power and control.

Feminists began to look for causes of male domination in societal institutions rather than in physical strength or biological instinct. From a feminist perspective, male-perpetrated violence against women is considered to be a form of social control used to maintain a subordinate social and political status for women. In general, feminists have emphasized the social construction of male violence, not the biology or pathology of the individual.

Another significant contribution of feminist theorizing has been a shift from viewing different forms of male violence against women as separate entities toward viewing violence against women as a unitary phenomenon and an outgrowth of male power and privilege. Feminist theorists continue to view partner violence as reflective of a larger patriarchal structure that functions to subordinate women. Major institutions (including criminal justice, health, military, athletic, and religious institutions) are seen as reflecting patriarchal values and encouraging and maintaining violence against women. A list of patriarchal values that have become institutionalized in our laws and cultural practices is found in Table 1.

Table 1: Patriarchal Values Related to Partner Violence

1. It is the natural, God-given right of men to have power over women.
2. The male head of a household should be in charge, hold all power, make the decisions, and be responsible for determining the actions and behaviors of those within the household.
3. Masculinity should be defined by powerful characteristics: strength, agency, independence, power, control, and domination.
4. Women pose a threat to male power and therefore need to be controlled. Femininity should be defined by weakness, passivity, dependence, powerlessness, and submissiveness.
5. Female sexuality is a particular threat to male power and therefore should be under the control of men, specifically fathers and/or husbands.
6. Sexual harassment, rape, physical violence, and any other fear-reducing tactics are legitimate and effective means to enforce male entitlements and to control women.

The Politics of Terminology

A key contribution of feminist analyses has been the development of more complex and sophisticated conceptualizations of multiple forms of violence. In addition to partner violence, these forms include rape, sexual abuse, torture, and sexual harassment. Male violence against women is ubiquitous—found in streets, homes, schools, and workplaces around the globe. It is directed also at female children, as in sexual abuse, incest, forced prostitution, and female infanticide.

Feminists have emphasized the importance of conceptualizing and naming violence in ways that reflect women's experiences. Labels that do not fully encompass physical, sexual, and psychological aspects of violence and/or gay and lesbian partner abuse, dating and cohabitation violence, and intimate violence occurring outside the home have important political implications. Such labels can exclude the experiences of some women and may downplay the role of men as perpetrators. For example, use of the terms *wife battering* and *marital violence* fails to recognize the large numbers of unmarried women or lesbian women who are assaulted by their sexual partners. The terms *intimate violence* and *domestic violence* do not specifically recognize women as targets and men as perpetrators. However such violence is defined and named, women are most likely to be the victims, particularly when the violence is severe. Here we speak of partner violence when referring to male violence against an intimate partner, whether married or unmarried.

In considering the experience of violence from the point of view of its victims, it must be recognized that threat of violence can be as effective as physical violence as a form of social control. Many feminists thus view acts experienced as threat, coercion, abuse, intimidation, or force used by men to control women as forms of violence. Thus, instances where the situation involves a threat of violence, such as stalking and sexual terrorism, are also forms of male violence against women.

Against Categorizing Male Violence

Although the model here focuses on partner violence, it must be kept in mind that male violence against women can take many forms, and treating these forms as discrete categories can mask the realities of violence in women's lives. Women who experienced childhood sexual abuse report higher rates of partner violence. Furthermore, dividing battering and rape into distinct and separate categories may obscure the overlapping nature of battery and rape in women's experiences. Similarly, separating violence in the home from violence in the workplace may be an artificial distinction that does not reflect actual experiences. Research on violence in the workplace has indicated that relationship or partner violence accounts for a sizable proportion of women who die on the job each year. Some feminist theorists have argued that it may be more helpful to think of violence against women as a continuum rather than as discrete categories. In this way, specific violent acts are viewed as part of a multidimensional continuum of gendered violence that acknowledges the diversity of women's experiences.

A Crosscutting Issue

Regardless of the form the violence takes, some common themes emerge from the literature on male-perpetrated violence. [M.P.] Koss, [L.] Heise, and [N.F.] Russo (1994) identified several common themes in the literature on battering, rape, and sexual harassment. First, regardless of the form violence takes, it is a pervasive, tenacious, everyday event in many women's lives, an event that crosses the lines of race, ethnicity, national origin, class, religion, age, and sexual orientation. In a comprehensive review of 52 studies, [G.T.] Hotaling and [D.B.] Sugarman (1986) found that income level, education level, social status, and individual personality characteristics did not influence a woman's chances for victimization. This suggests that women from all demographic backgrounds are at risk, and studies that cross lines of ethnicity, class, and other social categories are needed.

Although feminists have emphasized the importance of understanding the experiences of diverse women, there is still an inadequate understanding of violence in the lives of ethnic minority women. Fortunately, researchers are now beginning to investigate male perpetrated violence in African American, Native American, Hispanic American, and Asian American populations. In addition, international and cross-cultural studies are being conducted with female populations as diverse as refugees, central American immigrants, Ghanians, African Caribbeans, and women living in rural Papua, New Guinea.

Gender Construction and Society

Second, in all forms of violence between intimates, men are most likely to be the perpetrators and women are most likely to be the targets. This suggests that understanding gender-role constructions is key to predicting and preventing such violence. We need to know more about how these constructions vary—ethnicity, age, and region of the country are just a few examples of sources of variation in such constructions.

Third, understanding the relationship of violence to power dynamics is another key element of the picture. The sociocultural context shapes, fosters, and encourages the use of violence to maintain inequitable power relationships in the workplace, in the home, and in the community. Fourth, the majority of women who experience violence are abused by people in their daily environment—the people with whom they live and work. Whether the act of aggression involves harassment, rape, or assault, the perpetrator is often known to the victim. This suggests that relational expectations and scripts also play important roles in shaping and perpetuating violence.

Institutionalized Patriarchy

Fifth, our social institutions tend to trivialize and/or ignore women's experiences of violence. Coaches, judges, law enforcement officials, social service workers, religious leaders, teachers, and even mental health professionals have contributed to the prevailing cultural attitudes that serve to maintain and foster male violence. Our social structures themselves often reflect inequitable gender relationships that serve to maintain the legitimacy of male violence. Relationships between female workers and male employers, wives and husbands, female patients and male doctors, female athletes and male coaches, for example, share common structural and ideological features in which women are in positions of subordination to men. These inequities reinforce the patriarchal worldview that male domination over women is normal, natural, and expected.

Our health care systems, schools, workplaces, and courts exhibit systematic support for male violence against women on a daily basis. Specific to partner violence, the attitudes and practices of doctors indicate that many are failing to play a role in the prevention and treatment of men's violence against women. For example, partner violence often is ignored as a potential cause of problems in female patients seeking medical treatment in emergency rooms.

Our current legal and judicial systems enforce existing power relationships and thereby perpetuate partner violence. Studies of police response to partner violence indicate that levels of arrests are low, protection of women is often withheld, and the attitude of the state reflects a desire to stay out of family disputes and let the family members work the problems out privately. Some research suggests that police officers may openly discourage women from filing formal charges against a violent spouse. In one study of 1,870 partner violence reports over a 12-month period, less than 28% of cases ended in arrest. Although men were more likely to be identified as batterers, women identified as batterers were more likely to be charged with a serious crime. For example, black women were more likely to be arrested on felony charges (84%) than white men were (19%) for similar behavior. Even if the male perpetrator is arrested, there are additional biases and problems in our legal system. Legal outcomes in court cases of partner violence are highly dependent on the attitudes of individual judges rather than on firm legal standards. Investigations examining situations in which the justice system has failed to provide protection to female victims of partner violence have exposed several problems: the trivialization of women's experiences by law enforcement officials and judges, problems with arrest policies, and a common myth that both partners are equally responsible for the violent behavior. The inability of the criminal justice system to deal effectively with partner violence continues to be a major factor in the perpetuation of that violence.

Consequences for Victims

Sixth, feminists have exposed the destructive effects of male violence—to the woman, her family, and society. Women who have been victimized suffer both immediate and long range consequences to their physical and mental well-being, and these consequences are similar for multiple forms of victimization. Although many effects are immediately apparent following the violent episode(s), other effects may last for years or may surface as intermittent problems.

Victims of partner violence may suffer a variety of physical wounds including bruises, cuts, broken bones, loss of hearing or vision, burns, knife wounds, and even death. . . .

Effects of partner violence can extend beyond physical wounds to include a variety of psychological consequences. The aftereffects of partner violence may look very much like those experienced following any severe trauma—feelings of fearfulness, anxiety, confusion, anger, and powerlessness. Reactions of shock, denial, depression, and withdrawal also may occur. In one study, as the frequency and intensity of the abuse worsened, depressive symptomatology increased and self-esteem dropped. . . .

Not a Private Issue

In conclusion, feminists have emphasized that male violence against women is a complex, multifaceted phenomenon that takes multiple forms and is rooted in patriarchal social structures and cultural roles of women and men. Feminists have documented widespread and long-lasting effects of such violence to the woman, her family, and society, providing irrefutable justification for the argument that society cannot afford to define partner violence as a private issue. Understanding, predicting, and preventing such violence will require a complex and comprehensive approach that intervenes at individual, interpersonal, and structural levels.

"There is no direct relationship between structural patriarchy and wife assault."

Patriarchy Does Not Cause Domestic Violence

Charles E. Corry

Charles E. Corry is the president of the Equal Justice Foundation, a nonprofit organization concerned with maintaining the
rule of law and a social order that treats all people fairly. In the
following viewpoint, Corry responds to the argument that domestic violence results from men's desire to maintain patriarchal control over women. To Corry, such a theory ignores the
personal and psychological motives that underlie the problem
in male batterers and instead foists the blame onto an innate
condition within all men. Corry also counters the notion of patriarchy by illustrating that women worldwide have often been
found to commit more severe physical violence in their homes
and in their communities than men.

As you read, consider the following questions:

1. According to the author, what three conclusions does
   researcher D.G. Dutton offer to refute the notion that
   patriarchy causes domestic violence?
2. As cited by Corry, what overall conclusion do Sam and
   Bunny Sewell make about women and violence
   worldwide?
3. Corry refers to a 1988 Canadian study of domestic
   violence performed by Merlin Brinkerhoff and Eugen
   Lupri. According to that study, how many more times
   were women severely violent in domestic disputes than
   men?

patriarchy: 1. a form of social organization in which the father is the supreme authority in the family, clan, or tribe and descent is reckoned in the male line, with the children belonging to the father's clan or tribe. 2. a society, community, or country based on this social organization.

The Feminist Viewpoint

Gloria Steinem has asserted that "The patriarchy requires violence or the subliminal threat of violence in order to maintain itself. . . . The most dangerous situation for a woman is not an unknown man in the street, or even the enemy in wartime, but a husband or lover in the isolation of their own home."

Feminist analysis thus states that a patriarchal society is a direct cause of domestic violence against women.

Steinem's theory rests on such works as Robert Burns' 1788 poem:

The Henpecked Husband

Curs'd be the man, the poorest wretch in life,
The crouching vassal to a tyrant wife!
Who has no will but by her high permission,
Who has not sixpence but in her possession;
Who must to her, his dear friend's secrets tell,
Who dreads a curtain lecture worse than hell.
Were such the wife had fallen to my part,
I'd break her spirit or I'd break her heart;
I'd charm her with the magic of a switch,
I'd kiss her maids, and kick the perverse bitch.

Feminist theory thus renders the idea of therapy for men who assault their female partners as implausible because such behavior is "normal" in a patriarchal society. That unproven feminist theory has been translated into laws that forbid mediation in cases where domestic violence is alleged and require the forced separation of the man and woman regardless of their desires.

Men who abuse their mates, the theory goes, act violently not because they as individuals can't control their impulses, and not because they are thugs, or drunks, or particularly troubled people, but because such behavior is inherent in a patriarchy. Domestic abuse, in feminist eyes, is an essential element of the vast male conspiracy to suppress and subordinate women. To keep men from abusing women they must be taught to see the errors of the patriarchy and to renounce them.

Patricia Pearson points out: "That men have used a patriarchal vocabulary to account for themselves doesn't mean that patriarchy causes their violence, any more than being patriarchs prevents them from being victimized. Studies of male batterers have failed to confirm that these men are more conservative or sexist about marriage than nonviolent men. To the contrary, some of the highest rates of violence are found in the least orthodox partnerships—dating or cohabiting lovers."

In short, correlation does not imply causation, a fundamental theorem of statistics. Yet on the basis of this fundamental error, a multibillion dollar domestic violence industry has arisen to the detriment of families and civilization.

Women Are More Violent than Men

[D.G.] Dutton has examined the patriarch theory and rejects it for the following reasons:
- Battering in lesbian couples is much more frequent than heterosexual battering and lesbian relationships are significantly more violent than gay relationships.
- There is no direct correlation between how power is shared in a relationship and violence within couples.
- There is no direct relationship between structural patriarchy and wife assault.

Research to date indicates abuse and violence occurs in more than 50% of lesbian relationships compared to around 10% in other types of relationships. That would certainly not be true if domestic violence were in any way related to a patriarchal society.

There is evidence from a variety of sources that women are more violent in a domestic setting while men wage war globally.

The Revs. [Sam and Bunny] Sewell point out in their recent report that: "We think it is important to note that there have been the same kind of studies done in many countries. There is cross-cultural verification that women are more violent than men in family settings. When behavior has cross-cultural verification it means that it is part of human nature rather than a result of cultural conditioning. Females are most often the perpetrators in spousal violence in most cultures that have been studied to date. That leads many professionals to conclude that there is something biological about violent females in family situations. Researchers are now exploring the role of the 'territorial imperative' as a factor in women's violence against men. Women see the home as their territory. Like many other species on the planet, we humans will ignore size difference when we experience conflict on our own territory. So, the scientific results that reveal the violence of American women are not unique to our culture, and do not indicate a special pathology among American women. Worldwide, women are more violent than men in family settings."

Powerlessness and Control

Domestic violence, according to the prevailing zeitgeist, is about power and control, or more specifically, about the batterer's need to exert power and control over his female partner. The question of why some men have the need to exert power and control over their intimate partners is rarely, if ever, addressed. One logical answer is that they have the need to exert power and control over others because they feel impotent and powerless in their own lives. [G.R.] Brooks (1998) writing about traditional men, a population in which batterers are well represented, describes the fact that many men feel "powerless in their private lives" and notes that this is even more true of "underclass and marginalized men," who feel ashamed "about their inadequacy in relation to other men.". . .

Anecdotally, many batterers report having been victims of bullying and abuse as children. Especially among the angriest batterers, a history of being picked on, humiliated, or excluded is common. Further, they report that the perpetrators were not only peers or agemates, but in many cases were family members, including the parents. . . . This might not merely affect the batterer's self-esteem, and there is empirical evidence that they have impaired self-esteem, but could also be seen as contributing to their sense of powerlessness and hopelessness about the future. Power and control is more than a strategy, it is a human need.

Alan Rosenbaum and Penny A. Leisring, "Beyond Power and Control: Towards an Understanding of Partner Abusive Men," *Journal of Comparative Family Studies*, Winter 2003.

Susan Steinmetz, Ph.D., a leading researcher in the field of family violence, has done a cross-cultural comparison of marital abuse. Using a modified version of the Conflict Tactics Scale (CTS), she examined marital violence in small samples from six societies: Finland, United States, Canada, Puerto Rico, Belize, and Israel. Her results suggest that ". . . in each society the percentage of husbands who used violence was similar to the percentage of violent wives." The major exception was Puerto Rico where men were more violent. She also found that: "Wives who used violence . . . tended to use greater amounts."

A 1988 survey of couples in Canada by [Merlin] Brinkerhoff and [Eugen] Lupri found the same pattern. They examined interspousal violence in a representative sample of 562 couples in Calgary, Canada. They used the standard Conflict Tactics Scale and found twice as much severe violence where females assaulted males, 11%, as male assaulting female, 5%. The overall violence ratio for men was 10% while the overall violence ratio for women was 13%. Their study found significantly higher violence in younger and childless couples, and that male violence decreased with higher educational attainment while female violence increased.

Intent on Destroying Families

As she did with many issues, Erin Pizzey recognized very early that domestic violence had nothing to do with the patriarchy. In her book *Prone to Violence*, she compares violent men from the patriarchal society of Nigeria and the matriarchal society of West India and finds no basic differences. She has also argued that the feminist movement's intent is to destroy families as we know them.

The cross-cultural studies referenced above yielded results very similar to family violence studies done in the United States and other nations.

Conversely, there is considerable evidence that the feminist matriarchy has had considerable negative influence on domestic tranquility in the form of draconian Big Sister laws that forcefully separate men and women and are destroying families regardless of the individuals' wishes.

We are not aware of any matriarchal society that has independently developed beyond the Stone Age. While such societies readily use technology borrowed from patriarchal neighbors, if left alone matriarchal enclaves appear to quickly revert back to a Stone Age level. Haiti, and any inner city ghetto, would be modern examples.

"For young couples in their first year of marriage, there does seem to be an association between acute alcohol use on the part of the husband and the occurrence of domestic violence."

Alcohol Contributes to Domestic Violence

Kenneth E. Leonard and Brian M. Quigley

In the following viewpoint, Kenneth E. Leonard and Brian M. Quigley assert that acute alcohol consumption contributes to husband-on-wife spousal abuse. Using a study that tracked the occurrence of verbal threats and physical aggression among newlywed, heterosexual couples over their first three years of marriage, Leonard and Quigley found that alcohol was a determining factor in both the number of violent episodes and their severity. Although the authors acknowledge that more than half of the severely violent episodes reported did not involve alcohol, their study reveals that alcohol consumption was two to three times more prevalent in physical attacks than in verbal aggression. Kenneth E. Leonard and Brian M. Quigley are research scientists at the Research Institute on Addictions, part of the State University of New York at Buffalo.

As you read, consider the following questions:
1. According to the authors, what is the "proximal effects of alcohol model"?
2. How many couples took part in the newlywed study?
3. What are the four limitations that Leonard and Quigley admit might have an effect on their analysis?

Kenneth E. Leonard and Brian M. Quigley, "Drinking and Marital Aggression in Newlyweds: An Event-Based Analysis of Drinking and the Occurrence of Husband Marital Aggression," *Journal of Studies on Alcohol*, July 1999. Copyright © 1999 by the *Journal of Studies on Alcohol*. Reproduced by permission.

E xcessive alcohol consumption has been one of the most consistent correlates of domestic violence to emerge over the past two decades of research. Numerous studies have documented that the risk of marital violence is higher among men who drink excessively than among more moderate drinkers. Despite these relatively consistent findings, the causal significance of alcohol remains controversial. There are three basic explanations of the association between excessive drinking and domestic violence: the spurious model, the indirect effects model, and the proximal effects of alcohol model. The spurious model maintains that excessive drinking is related to domestic violence by virtue of its association with other factors that influence both the drinking and the violence. The indirect effects model suggests that heavy drinking creates an unhappy, conflict ridden marital environment, and that it is this context, rather than drinking per se, that is proximally associated with domestic violence. While spurious factors and indirect pathways undoubtedly contribute to the relationship between alcohol and domestic violence, studies controlling for these factors have nonetheless observed significant relationships between alcohol and domestic violence. The third model for explaining the relationship between drinking patterns and domestic violence is the proximal effects of alcohol model. According to this approach, men who maintain patterns of excessive drinking are more likely to engage in domestic violence or to engage in more severe domestic violence because they are often intoxicated and alcohol intoxication facilitates violence. This facilitative effect may be mediated through the psychopharmacologic effects of alcohol on cognitive processing or the expectancy or excuse functions of intoxication. Despite the prominence of this approach, evidence regarding this model has been limited to experimental studies of alcohol and laboratory aggression and reports of the prevalence of alcohol use in domestic violence. . . .

Few studies have addressed the issue of whether acute alcohol consumption is related to either the occurrence or severity of domestic violence. In an early study, [M.] Bard and [J.] Zacker (1974) trained police officers in observation and data recording during family disturbances. Officers reported on 962 families involved in 1,388 disputes that required police intervention. Among those instances in which an assault was judged to have occurred, 21% were reported to involve alcohol use. Among the nonassaultive episodes, 40% were reported to involve alcohol. This difference was significant and suggested that alcohol use may have prevented violence. [J.A.] Fagan and associates (1983) interviewed 270 women, who had previously been involved in domestic violence intervention programs, about the violent event that brought them into contact with the program. Although alcohol use was common in the episodes, it was unrelated to the extent of injury that each woman experienced in this event. However, the alcohol use variable was not whether alcohol was present in the event, but instead the extent to which alcohol was present in all episodes of violence. [K.] Pernanen (1991) interviewed a random community sample about their most recent victimization. Focusing on a small subsample of domestic violence cases, he found that 13% of victims of sober violence were injured while 26% of victims of intoxicated violence were injured. This difference was not significant, possibly due to a relatively small sample of subjects whose last victimization was from a spouse. [S.E.] Martin and [R.] Bachman (1997) utilized data from the National Crime Victimization Survey for 1992 and 1993 to determine whether assault severity was associated with drinking or drug use by the assailant. Severity was defined as a three-category variable of threat, assault without injury, and assault with injury. Focusing on the instances of intimate violence toward women, a significant association between assailant alcohol use and severity was observed: 54% of alcohol-involved assaults were severe (i.e., assault with injury), but only 43% of the sober assaults were severe. Moreover, this association remained significant after controlling for victim marital status and age, and whether or not the incident took place in a public place. In summary, the evidence to date that acute alcohol use is involved with either the occurrence or severity of domestic violence has been equivocal.

The above studies utilized a between-groups strategy for examining the role of situational variables in the occurrence of target events. In this approach, individuals who have experienced a specific target event, for example, an actual assault, are contrasted with different individuals who have experienced a similar, but less serious target event, for example, a verbal threat. These different individuals then describe the situational factors, such as whether the assailant was drinking, that accompanied the index event. For such a comparison to be informative one must take into account that the individuals who experienced the different events are not necessarily comparable and that other situational factors might differ between the two types of events. . . .

A second event-based strategy involves collecting different kinds of target events from the same individuals. For example, one might collect situational information from two different events—an instance of verbal threat that did not involve physical aggression and an instance of physical aggression—from individuals who had experienced both. While it would still be necessary to demonstrate that the other situational factors were comparable, the fact that the participants serve as their own control obviates the need to control for individual difference factors. . . .

The Buffalo Newlywed Study

The purpose of the present study is to examine the role of husband and wife drinking in marital aggressive events using both the between-groups and within-groups strategies. For the between-groups analysis, we compare the presence of drinking among couples whose most serious marital conflict was either an argument, moderate physical aggression or serious physical aggression while controlling for key background factors including drinking patterns and marital conflict and situational factors. For the within-groups analyses, we examine a subset of husbands and wives who reported on both a verbal argument and an instance of physical aggression. It was hypothesized that husband alcohol use at the time of the event would be associated with the severity of the episode, with a higher prevalence of drinking in serious than in less serious events. The role of wife's drinking was also explored. . . .

This study is based on a subsample of 366 couples who participated in the Buffalo Newlywed Study (BNS) conducted at the Research Institute on Addictions in Buffalo,

NY. The BNS is a three-wave longitudinal study of newly-wed couples with assessments at the time of marriage (TO), at the first anniversary (T+1) and at the third anniversary (T+3). The current subsample consists of couples that provided complete data at TO and were interviewed in person at T+1. The mean age at marriage for husbands was 24.2 (range = 18–29) and for wives was 23.3 (range = 15–36). The sample was largely white (73% of husbands and 75% of wives). Blacks were represented in approximately the same proportion as in the urban area from which couples were recruited (23% of husbands and 22% of wives). With respect to education, 10% of husbands and 7% of wives did not graduate from high school and 28% of husbands and 23% of wives were high school graduates. Approximately 36% of the husbands and 43% of the wives reported having some education beyond high school, but not graduating (some of these were still in school). Slightly more than a quarter of husbands and wives (25% of husbands and 28% of wives) were college graduates. The majority of the subjects were employed, 87% of husbands and 68% of wives. Reflecting the demographic composition of the area they were recruited from, a majority of the couples were Catholic (60% of husbands and 61% of wives).

BNS couples were first approached at a marriage license bureau as they applied for their marriage license. Couples who indicated that this was the first marriage for both husband and wife and that the husband was between the ages of 18 and 29, inclusive, were requested to participate in a brief screening interview for which the couple received $5. The spouses were then given questionnaire packets and separate postage-paid envelopes and told that they each would receive $25 for completing and returning the questionnaires. The couples were instructed to complete the questionnaires in private, return them within 2 weeks, and not to discuss the questionnaires until both of them had completed and mailed them back. Over the course of the study, 76% of the couples who were approached participated in the screening; among successfully screened subjects, complete questionnaire data from both spouses were collected from 647 couples, or approximately 77% of the couples who agreed to participate.

All couples, whether or not they provided complete data at the initial assessment (TO), were recontacted at the 1-year anniversary of their marriage (T+1). At the T+1 assessment, couples were asked to complete the same questionnaires completed at the time of marriage. Each member of the couple then participated in an extensive in-person interview with a same-sex interviewer that focused on the occurrences of verbal and physical aggression in the first year of marriage. Husbands and wives were interviewed separately. Couples who were unable or unwilling to participate in the in-person interview completed the questionnaires at home and participated in a telephone interview that assessed the occurrence of marital violence and whether the husband had been drinking. Situational information regarding verbal arguments and physical aggression was not collected in this brief interview. Consequently, the focus of the present analysis is 366 husbands and wives who participated in the in-person interview at T+1. . . .

First Anniversary Assessment

Husband's alcohol use. Because of the importance of controlling for patterns of alcohol use in the analysis of alcohol in the event, we included both husband and wife drinking and included four different aspects of alcohol consumption. A standard quantity-frequency measure was administered to assess participants' daily alcohol consumption over the past year (average daily volume, or ADV). The participants were also administered the Alcohol Dependence Scale (ADS). The ADS measures loss of behavior control regarding alcohol, obsessive-compulsive drinking, and psychoperceptual and psychophysical withdrawal from alcohol. We also utilized two items that assessed the frequency with which the individual had consumed six or more drinks in one setting, and the frequency with which the individual had drunk to intoxication.

Marital aggression. A modified version of the CTS [Conflict Tactics Scale] [a system used to rank the severity of aggressive behavior] was administered to both members of the couple at the T+1 interview to assess husband aggression. The version included verbal aggression (i.e., insulted or swore at partner, called her names, did or said something to spite her, yelled and screamed at her, and argued angrily), and moderate (i.e., throw something; push, grab or shove; slap) to severe physical aggression items (i.e., kicked; hit with a fist; hit or tried to hit with an object; beat up). After ascertaining the number of verbal aggression episodes, the participants were asked to focus on the most serious verbal conflict that did not involve physical aggression. Participants were asked questions concerning this conflict, including where it had occurred, whether other individuals were present, whether anyone attempted to intervene, and whether the participant or the participant's partner had been drinking prior to the episode. Those participants who indicated an occurrence of husband to wife physical aggression were then asked the same series of questions about the first and the most serious episodes.

For the between-groups analysis of events, this interview was utilized to develop the following measures: (1) the severity of the most severe event with three different levels, verbal aggression, mild physical aggression (push, grab or shove) and serious physical aggression (slap, hit with fist, beat up); (2) the husband's use of alcohol in the most severe event; (3) the wife's use of alcohol in the most severe event; (4) the presence of others during the most severe event; and (5) the location of the most severe event (in home versus out of home). These variables were constructed separately for husband report and wife report.

For the within-groups analysis, participants with both verbal aggression and at least one episode of physical aggression were considered. For this analysis, we constructed the following variables separately for the most serious verbal event and for the most serious physical event: the husband's use of alcohol, the wife's use of alcohol, the presence of others during the event, and the location of the event (in home versus out of home). . . .

Between-Groups Analysis

Across all three event types (i.e., verbal aggression, mild physical aggression, severe physical aggression), husbands reported that they were drinking in 10.8% of episodes and their wives were drinking in 11.4% of the episodes. There was a strong relationship between husband and wife drinking. . . . According to wife report, 18.9% of husbands and 5.9% of wives were drinking in the episode. As with husband report, there was a strong association between report of wife drinking and report of husband drinking. . . .

Situational Factors Among Participants with Verbal, Moderate Physical, or Severe Physical Aggression Episodes

Degree of Violence as Reported by Husband

Alcohol involved	Verbal (218 instances)	Moderate (45 instances)	Severe (61 instances)
Husband only	0.0%	8.9%	26.2%
Wife only	8.3%	0.0%	6.6%
Both	3.2%	2.2%	11.5%
Total husband	3.2%	11.1%	37.7%
Total wife	11.5%	2.2%	18.1%

Degree of Violence as Reported by Wife

Alcohol involved	Verbal (211 instances)	Moderate (44 instances)	Severe (67 instances)
Husband only	7.1%	25.0%	28.4%
Wife only	0.5%	0.0%	3.0%
Both	2.4%	2.3%	14.9%
Total husband	9.5%	27.3%	43.3%
Total wife	2.9%	2.3%	17.9%

This research was supported by National Institute on Alcohol Abuse and Alcoholism grant AA-07183 awarded to Kenneth E. Leonard.

Received: June 6, 1997. Revision: October 1, 1997.

Research Institute on Addictions, 1021 Main St., Buffalo, NY 14203.

Husbands reported that they were drinking (either husband only or both husband and wife) in 3.2% of verbal episodes, in 11.1% of moderate physical episodes and 37.7% of severe physical episodes. . . . Husbands indicated that their wives were drinking in 11.5% of verbal episodes, 2.2% of moderate physical episodes and 18.1% of severe physical episodes. . . . According to wife report, husbands were drinking in 9.5% of verbal episodes, 27.3% of moderate physical episodes and 43.3% of severe physical episodes. . . . Finally, wife report of her own drinking indicated that wife was drinking in 2.9% of verbal episodes, 2.3% of moderate physical events and 17.9% of severe physical events. . . .

As discussed previously, there are different participants reporting on different event types, and the above associations could be due to individual difference factors that relate to both aggression and the likelihood of alcohol consumption. Alternatively, other contextual factors could account for the relationship. . . .

Within-Subjects Analysis

For participants who reported both a verbal and a physical aggression episode, the extent to which husband and wife drinking were reported in these two events was examined. . . . The overall alcohol involvement reported in physical aggression (30.7% for husband report and 40.8% for wife report) was nearly twice the level reported in verbal aggression (16.9% for husband report and 21.3% for wife report).

In order to determine whether the use of alcohol was more prevalent in physical versus verbal aggression, the McNemar Test for significance of changes was used. Four separate contingency tables were constructed and evaluated. Husband report of husband drinking indicated a marginally greater involvement of alcohol in physical (26.7%) versus verbal episodes (15.9%). . . . Wife report of husband drinking indicated that alcohol was significantly more involved in physical (39%) than verbal episodes (20.4%). . . . Analyses of wife drinking in physical (10.9%) and verbal episodes (5%) failed to reveal a significant effect for husband report. . . . However, according to wife report, the wives were more likely to be drinking in the physical episodes (12%) than in the verbal aggression episodes (3.7%). . . .

Because the above differences could be attributed to contextual difference between verbal and physical episodes, the location of the episode and presence of other people were compared for physical and verbal episodes. Verbal and physical episodes were equally likely to occur in the home . . . and equally likely to occur in the presence of others. . . . Given that these variables were not differentially present in verbal versus physical episodes, the relationship between drinking and the nature of the episode cannot be attributed to them.

An Established Link

It is fairly well established that alcohol use frequently accompanies domestic violence. However, whether this association represents a causal relationship is still controversial. One of the key aspects of this controversy has been the absence of data linking alcohol use at the time of a domestic violence episode with the actual occurrence or severity of the violence. The present study found an association between husband drinking and the occurrence of an episode of physical versus verbal aggression. This finding was significant for both husband and wife reports and for two different methodologic approaches. In both of these methodologic approaches, individual differences that might create a spurious relationship between alcohol use and the occurrence of domestic violence were controlled, statistically in the between-groups analyses and by design in the within-groups analyses. Consequently, for young couples in their first year of marriage, there does seem to be an association between acute alcohol use on the part of the husband and the occurrence of domestic violence.

Although the findings were clear and consistent regarding husband drinking and the occurrence of domestic violence, the relationship between wife drinking and the occurrence of violence was not consistent across reporter or method. . . .

There were too few participants that reported on two episodes of violence to examine drinking and severity in the within-subjects framework. In the between-subjects analyses, there was some support for an association between husband drinking and severity. Husband drinking was associated with severe rather than moderate aggression, but only by husband's report. This effect was only marginal after controlling for wife drinking. While this provides tentative support for a link between husband drinking and husband violence, the failure to find significant effects according to wife report raises the possibility that the finding reflects husband reporting bias. Wife drinking was marginally associated with severe rather than moderate violence but only after controlling for husband drinking and only according to wife report. The most appropriate conclusion would be that there is little evidence that wife drinking is associated with husband aggression. . . .

Although the findings support an association between acute alcohol use and the occurrence and to some extent the severity of violence, it is important to recognize that these findings do not indicate that drinking is either a necessary or sufficient cause of violence. More than 50% of the severe episodes did not involve husband drinking. For moderate episodes, between 72.7% (by wife report) and 89.1% (by husband report) did not involve husband drinking. This finding mirrors findings reported by [K.G.] Kaufman-Kantor et al. (1990) that the husband was not drinking in 78% of aggressive episodes. Taken together, these studies support a more limited, contributory role for drinking in marital violence.

Limitations

There are several limitations to this study that warrant discussion. First, because this study was based on the second wave of longitudinal study, there was a moderate amount of attrition, and the attrition was not random. There was evidence that the heaviest drinkers were more likely to drop out than lighter drinkers, and this was true for both husbands and wives. There was also some attrition due to our inability to conduct the detailed interview over the telephone with participants who could not or would not come in. However, there is little evidence that this loss of subjects created a bias. A second limitation was the focus on husband-to-wife violence. As others have reported, the overall prevalence of specific aggressive actions is comparable for the wives and the husbands. However, given the evidence that men's aggression has a more significant impact than wives' aggression, we chose to examine episodes of husband aggression. A third limitation concerns the use of a 1-year retrospective self-report. It is possible that participants were unwilling to provide candid answers to the interview, or were unable to recall clearly the circumstances surrounding the violence. To be conservative, the small number of subjects who indicated that they didn't know whether they or their spouse was drinking in the event were treated as not drinking. More importantly, the replication of the basic finding across husband and wife report and across two different methodologies does minimize the concern with the self-report approach. Finally, it is important to note that this study does not necessarily indicate that drinking is a cause of marital violence. Instead, the study suggests that husband drinking is more prevalent in physical aggression than in verbal aggression episodes, and that this association cannot be attributed to personality factors or to the measured contextual factors.

In conclusion, the results of the present study strongly support an association between husband drinking and the occurrence of marital aggression, but not between wife drinking and the occurrence of aggression. With regard to the severity of aggression, there was some suggestion that wife drinking, primarily in the context of both husband and wife drinking, was associated with more severe episodes. These findings, though by no means definitive, are consistent with the view that alcohol consumption, either through its symbolic or psychopharmacologic properties, contribute to the occurrence and severity of marital violence among newlyweds.

"The majority of men are not high-level drinkers and the majority of men classified as high-level drinkers do not abuse their partners."

Alcohol Does Not Contribute to Domestic Violence

Theresa M. Zubretsky and Karla M. Digirolamo

In the following article, Theresa M. Zubretsky and Karla M. Digirolamo insist that alcohol is not a major contributor to most instances of domestic violence. They note that many aspects of domestic violence—such as economic control and intimidation—are in no way related to alcohol. The authors criticize treatment strategies that consider alcohol as a cause of domestic violence because this implies that curing the substance abuse will end the violence. To remedy this misconception, the authors suggest that substance abuse programs and domestic violence services coordinate their efforts to aid batterers and their victims. Zubretsky is the director of the Safety Zone, an organization that trains professionals in issues relating to chemically involved battered women. Digirolamo is the associate director of Unity House, a multipurpose human service agency. Both facilities are located in New York.

As you read, consider the following questions:
1. How do Zubretsky and Digirolamo define the "disinhibition theory"?
2. According to the authors, what effect does the recovery phase of drug addiction often have on domestic abuse?

Theresa M. Zubretsky and Karla M. Digirolamo, "The False Connection Between Adult Domestic Violence and Alcohol," *Helping Battered Women: New Perspectives and Remedies*, edited by Albert R. Roberts. New York: Oxford University Press, 1996. Copyright © 1996 by Oxford University Press. Reproduced by permission.

Since the 1970's, significant efforts have been made to increase the public's understanding of domestic violence and to educate professionals and service providers about this problem. Through accounts from battered and formerly battered women, domestic violence is now understood to include a range of behaviors—physical, sexual, economic, emotional and psychological abuse—directed toward establishing and maintaining power and control over an intimate partner. There is also an increased awareness that the societal tendency to blame domestic violence victims and excuse perpetrators is rooted in a history of cultural and legal traditions that have supported the domination and abuse of women by men in intimate relationships. Despite greater public awareness, however, myths and misconceptions about battered women's experiences persist. Interventions based on these myths can have a devastating effect on victims and their families.

Despite the significant correlation between domestic violence and chemical dependency, hardly any research has been conducted and little has been written about the need to develop intervention strategies that address both the domestic violence and the substance abuse problems of chemically dependent men who batter. Similarly, little has been done to assist battered women with chemical dependency problems to meet their need for both safety and sobriety. Neither system currently is equipped to provide the range of services needed by battered women and batterers who are affected by chemical dependency. In the addictions treatment system, misinformation often leads counselors to understand and respond to domestic violence through the use of an addictions framework, an approach that has particularly harmful consequences for battered women. Such an approach identifies battering either as a symptom of alcohol abuse or addiction or as an addiction itself. The interventions that follow are based on a number of *harmful, false assumptions:*

- Alcohol use and/or alcoholism causes men to batter.
- Alcoholism treatment alone will address the abuse adequately.
- Battered women are "co-dependent" and thus contribute to the continuation of abuse.

- Addicted battered women must get sober before they can begin to address their victimization.

Relationship of Alcohol Use to Violence

The belief that alcoholism causes domestic violence is a notion widely held both in and outside of the substance abuse field, despite a lack of information to support it. Although research indicates that among men who drink heavily, there is a higher rate of perpetrating assaults resulting in serious physical injury than exists among other men, the majority of men are not high-level drinkers and the majority of men classified as high-level drinkers do not abuse their partners.

Even for batterers who do drink, there is little evidence to suggest a clear pattern that relates the drinking to the abusive behavior. The majority (76 percent) of physically abusive incidents occur in the absence of alcohol use, and there is no evidence to suggest that alcohol use or dependence is linked to the other forms of coercive behaviors that are part of the pattern of domestic violence. Economic control, sexual violence, and intimidation, for example, are often part of a batterer's ongoing pattern of abuse, with little or no identifiable connection to his use of or dependence on alcohol.

The belief that alcoholism causes domestic violence evolves both from a lack of information about the nature of this abuse and from adherence to the "disinhibition theory." This theory suggests that the physiological effects of alcohol include a state of lowered inhibitions in which an individual can no longer control his behavior. Research conducted within the alcoholism field, however, suggests that the most significant determinant of behavior after drinking is not the physiological effect of the alcohol itself, but the expectation that individuals place on the drinking experience. When cultural norms and expectations about male behavior after drinking include boisterous or aggressive behaviors, for example, research shows that individual men are more likely to engage in such behaviors when under the influence than when sober.

Despite the research findings, the belief that alcohol lowers inhibitions persists and along with it, a historical tradition of holding people who commit crimes while under the influence of alcohol or other drugs less accountable than those who commit crimes in a sober state. Batterers, who have not been held accountable for their abusive behavior in general, find themselves even less accountable for battering perpetrated when they are under the influence of alcohol. The alcohol provides a ready and socially acceptable excuse for their violence.

Evolving from the belief that alcohol or substance abuse causes domestic violence is the belief that treatment for the chemical dependency will stop the violence. Battered women with drug-dependent partners, however, consistently report that during recovery the abuse not only continues, but often escalates, creating greater levels of danger than existed prior to their partners' abstinence. In the cases in which battered women report that the level of physical abuse decreases, they often report a corresponding increase in other forms of coercive control and abuse—the threats, manipulation and isolation intensify.

Power and Control, Not "Loss of Control"

The provision of appropriate services for families affected by domestic violence and substance abuse is further complicated by the belief that battering itself is addictive behavior. This belief may arise in part from an attempt to explain why violence often increases in severity over time. The progressive nature of the violence is likened to the progressive nature of the disease of addiction, inviting the use of an addictions model for responding to the problem of battering.

An addictions framework assumes that there is a point at which a batterer can no longer control his abuse, just as an addict experiences loss of control over the substance use. The experiences of battered women, however, challenge this view. Battered women report that even when their partners appear "uncontrollably drunk" during a physical assault, they routinely exhibit the ability to "sober up" remarkably quickly if there is an outside interruption, such as police intervention.

Batterers also exhibit control over the nature and extent of the physical violence they perpetrate, often directing their assaults to parts of their partners' bodies that are covered by clothing. Conversely, some batterers purposefully target their partners' faces to compel isolation or to disfigure them so that "no one else will want them." Batterers can articulate their personal limits regarding physical abuse, reporting, for example, that while they have slapped their partners with an open hand, they would never punch them with their fists. Others admit to hitting and punching but report that they would never use a weapon.

Alcohol's Spurious Link to Violence

It has been argued . . . that violence against wives occurs within a context of coercive control and varies in relation to threats to male dominance and feelings of entitlement over female partners. The results of [our 2000] study indicate that male attitudes supportive of the rightness of control and subjugation of female partners made a more important statistical contribution to predictions about violence than did alcohol abuse, age, type of relationship, or class variables. The acting out of negative attitudes toward women, especially men's rights to degrade and devalue their female partners through name-calling and put-downs, were especially important predictors and, once entered into the model, reduced the effects of alcohol abuse to non-significance. Name-calling and put-downs was the single most important predictor of violence, net of the effects of all others in the model.

This study lends support to the theories of [J.W.] Messerschmidt (1993) and [M.] Schwartz & [W.] Dekeseredy (1997) that young males look to both alcohol and to the control of and violence against female partners to enhance their masculine status. This suggests that the link between alcohol and violence may indeed be a spurious one in which masculinity is acted out through both heavy drinking and attacks and degradation of female partners. The effects of both age and alcohol as predictors of violence were reduced significantly when evidence of negative attitudes toward women was taken into account, although age remained important.

Holly Johnson, "The Role of Alcohol in Male Partners' Assaults on Wives," *Journal of Drug Issues*, Fall 2000.

The escalation in the severity of violence over time does not represent a batterer's "loss of control" over the violence, as the analogy to addictions would suggest. Instead, violence may get worse over time because increasing the intensity of the abuse is an effective way for batterers to maintain their control over their partners and prevent them from leaving. The violence may also escalate because most batterers experience few, if any, negative consequences for their abusive behavior. Social tolerance of domestic violence thus not only contributes to its existence, but may also influence its progression and batterers' definitions of the acceptable limits of their abuse.

Interventions with Substance-Abusing Batterers

Batterers who are also alcohol or other drug involved need to address both problems separately and concurrently. This is critical not only to maximize the victim's safety, but also to prevent the battering from precipitating relapse or otherwise interfering with the recovery process. True recovery requires much more than abstinence. It includes adopting a lifestyle that enhances one's emotional and spiritual health, a goal that cannot be achieved if the battering continues.

Self-help programs such as Alcoholics Anonymous promote and support emotional and spiritual health and have helped countless numbers of alcoholics get sober. These programs, however, were not designed to address battering and are insufficient in motivating batterers to stop their abuse. Accordingly, a treatment plan for chemically dependent men who batter must include attendance at programs designed specifically to address the attitudes and beliefs that support batterers' behavior.

Impact of Co-Dependency Treatment on Battered Women

Most often, the partners of batterers in chemical dependency treatment are themselves directed into self-help programs such as Al-Anon or co-dependency groups. Like other traditional treatment responses, however, these resources were not designed to meet the needs of victims of domestic violence and often inadvertently cause harm to battered women.

The goals of Al-Anon and co-dependency treatment typically include helping family members of alcoholics to get "self-focused," practice emotional detachment from the substance abusers, and identify and stop their enabling or "co-dependent" behaviors, that is, to stop protecting their partners from the harmful consequences of addiction. Group members are encouraged to define their personal boundaries, set limits on their partners' behaviors, and stop protecting their partners from the harmful consequences of the addiction. While these strategies and goals may be very useful for women whose partners are not batterers, for battered women such changes will likely result in an escalation of abuse, including physical violence.

Battered women are often very attuned to their partners' moods as a way to assess their level of danger. They focus on their partners' needs and "cover up" for them as part of their survival strategy. Battered women's behaviors are not symptomatic of some underlying "dysfunction," but are the life-saving skills necessary to protect them and their children from further harm. When battered women are encouraged to stop these behaviors through self-focusing and detachment, they are, in essence, being asked to stop doing the things that may be keeping them and their children most safe.

Battered women whose partners are chemically dependent should be given accurate and complete information about available resources so that they can make informed choices and set realistic expectations about the potential benefits of these different sources of help. It is critical that they understand the purposes of Al-Anon and co-dependency groups and the limitations of these forums as sources of accurate information regarding safety-related concerns. They should also be advised of the availability of local domestic violence programs and referred to these services for assistance. Empowering women with accurate information will help them make decisions that best meet their individual needs.

Chemically Dependent Battered Women

Although the vast majority of battered women are not alcohol or substance abusers, those who are confront a system that is ill-equipped to deal with their needs, particularly their need for safety. Often, intakes to treatment programs do not include an assessment for adult domestic violence. Even when domestic violence is identified, it is often assumed that treatment for the substance abuse must occur before the victimization can be addressed.

One of the concerns with the "sobriety first" approach is that it does not consider the increased risk of violence that a woman's recovery may precipitate. Batterers often are resistant to their partners' attempts to seek help of any kind, including substance abuse treatment. In response, they may sabotage the recovery process by preventing victims from attending meetings or keeping appointments, or they may increase the violence in order to reestablish control. Many chemically dependent battered women leave treatment in response to the increased danger or are otherwise unable to comply with treatment demands because of the obstacles constructed by their partners. Even if a battered woman is able to complete a treatment program, being revictimized is predictive of relapse.

An additional concern with the "sobriety first" approach is that it does not recognize the relationship between the substance use and a battered woman's victimization. Many battered women report that they began to use substances as a way to cope with unremitting danger and fear. Often, these women report that they had sought help repeatedly from the traditional social service and legal systems, but received inadequate or negative responses. In fact, many chemically dependent battered women are addicted to sedatives, tranquilizers, stimulants and hypnotics, drugs that were prescribed by the health care providers from whom they sought help.

Whatever the drug of choice, substance-using battered women often report that the substances helped them cope with their fear and manage the daily activities of their lives in the face of ongoing abuse and danger. These are women who may be particularly resistant to engaging in a recovery process until they are confident that they can achieve genuine safety from the violence. For these women, an intervention framework that requires "sobriety first" is an approach that is almost destined to fail.

Lack of Information in Domestic Violence Field

Traditional addictions treatment approaches are insufficient to meet the needs of battered women, both those whose partners are addicted and those who themselves have a substance abuse problem. In many ways, the services typically provided by the domestic violence service system are equally inadequate to meet the needs of women affected by both problems.

Chemically dependent battered women often have very limited or no access to safe shelter through the emergency domestic violence shelter network because of their addiction. While admission and discharge policies must consider the safety needs of all shelter residents, policies that prohibit access by chemically dependent battered women and that often are based on misconceptions about addiction, cut off many women from a vital resource. Even when admission criteria do not categorically exclude chemically dependent battered women from services, domestic violence programs do not conduct appropriate screening for substance abuse and regularly fail even to minimally evaluate the addiction treatment needs of sheltered battered women.

Despite the fact that domestic violence programs do not adequately assess battered women for substance abuse problems, these programs do refer women to chemical dependency treatment agencies more frequently than the reverse occurs, suggesting to some that domestic violence programs have a greater desire to forge cooperative relationships with these providers of substance abuse treatment. There are, however, alternative explanations that may account for the high referral rates by domestic violence programs. The lack of information and training on chemical dependency among domestic violence program staff and/or the existence of harmful attitudes and beliefs about chemically dependent women may impede the direct provision of supportive and empowering interventions by domestic violence advocates. The subsequent referrals may then become a way to shift difficult cases to another agency or to someone else's caseload. Advocates often miss an important opportunity to interrupt the deadly progression of women's alcohol or other drug addictions, problems that may significantly impair battered women's efforts to get safe.

Creating an Effective Partnership

Meeting the needs of battered women who are affected by substance abuse requires an effective working relationship between the two service systems, a need consistently identified by workers in both fields, but an undertaking fraught with multiple obstacles to cooperation. The battered women's movement is a grassroots social change movement based on a socio-political analysis of domestic violence. The alcoholism field works from a medical model and provides treatment from a perspective that understands chemical dependency as a disease. The subsequent conflicts that emerge in attempts to coordinate services to individuals affected by both problems are predictable and legitimate. The differences in language and approach reflect the analyses and perspectives of two very different problems. They are differences, however, that can and must be reconciled.

Despite the disparities, both the substance abuse and domestic violence service systems are combating problems that each day threaten the lives and well-being of countless women, children, and men. Both systems are battling barriers rooted in social attitudes and traditions that interfere with the provision of effective services and that frequently lead to harmful responses to those seeking help. It is essential that providers work together to ensure that our respective responses promote victim safety, offender accountability, and recovery from addiction.

> *"Intimate partner violence is entirely a product of its social context. Consequently, understanding the causes of such violence requires research in many social contexts."*

Domestic Violence Has Many Causes

Rachel Jewkes

In the following viewpoint, Rachel Jewkes asserts that there are many causal factors associated with domestic violence. Among these are poverty, alcohol consumption, learned behavior patterns, and increased female independence. Although the latter factor often provides women with a way to escape intimate violence, female independence can sometimes result in violence by males attempting to retain dominance and control of their partners. In fact, Jewkes argues that many of the risk factors are in some way related to an upset of traditional gender roles in specific societies. Rachel Jewkes is director of the Medical Research Council of South Africa's Women's Health Research Unit. She wrote the following article for the *Lancet*, an international medical journal.

As you read, consider the following questions:

1. What three household characteristics does Jewkes say are not related to intimate partner violence?
2. According to the author, how does women's education confer empowerment in relation to domestic violence?
3. What is the intergenerational cycle of violence, as defined by Jewkes?

Rachel Jewkes, "Intimate Partner Violence: Causes and Prevention," *The Lancet*, April 20, 2002. Copyright © 2002 by Elsevier Science Publishers, Ltd. Reproduced by permission.

Unlike many health problems, there are few social and demographic characteristics that define risk groups for intimate partner violence. Poverty is the exception and increases risk through effects on conflict, women's power, and male identity. Violence is used as a strategy in conflict. Relationships full of conflict, and especially those in which conflicts occur about finances, jealousy, and women's gender role transgressions are more violent than peaceful relationships. Heavy alcohol consumption also increases risk of violence. Women who are more empowered educationally, economically, and socially are most protected, but below this high level the relation between empowerment and risk of violence is non-linear. Violence is frequently used to resolve a crisis of male identity, at times caused by poverty or an inability to control women. Risk of violence is greatest in societies where the use of violence in many situations is a socially accepted norm. Primary preventive interventions should focus on improving the status of women and reducing norms of violence, poverty, and alcohol consumption.

Difficulty in Finding Plausible Links

Poverty or patriarchy, alcohol or aggression; the causes of intimate partner violence have been contested by social scientists for decades. Underlying the controversy is an inescapable problem: evidence for causation of intimate partner violence is weak when assessed with epidemiological criteria. Most research has been from North America and, with some exceptions, has been based on women accessing sources of help, with data obtained from shelters, official records, or clinic samples. However, during the past decade, the research base has been expanded substantially by several well designed cross-sectional studies of violence against women from developing countries, which focus on both women and men, and by ethnographic studies. This increase in data has enabled researchers to identify associations that pertain to more than one setting, explore hypotheses critically, and understand the plausibility of associations when considered in the light of what else is known about a society. Furthermore, understanding of the mechanisms through which many associated factors contribute to intimate partner violence has been greatly advanced, helping clarify interventions needed for primary prevention.

Understanding the causes of intimate partner violence is substantially more difficult than studying a disease. For example, diseases usually have a biological basis and occur within a social context, but intimate partner violence is entirely a product of its social context. Consequently, understanding the causes of such violence requires research in many social contexts. Most diseases can be investigated with various objective measures, but measurement of intimate partner violence has posed a challenge. Furthermore, measurement of social conditions thought to be risk factors, such as the status of women, gender norms, and socioeconomic status poses difficulties, especially across cultures. Although a consensus has emerged on the need to explore male and female factors and aspects of the dynamics of relationships, this has been done in very few studies. Additionally, the validity of research on sensitive topics is dependent on the context of the interview and good interviewer training. Interviewer effects can be substantial. Researchers have only recently begun to use a multilevel approach in analyses that allows for interviewer effects.

In this [viewpoint], intimate partner violence describes physical violence directed against a woman by a current or ex-husband or boyfriend. The term "intimate partner violence" often includes sexual violence and can also include psychological abuse; both these forms of abuse often, but not always, accompany physical violence. However, inconsistencies in the definitions used in research, particularly with regard to inclusion or exclusion of sexual and psychological abuse by male intimate partners, has resulted in most global quantitative studies on the causes of intimate partner violence focusing solely on physical violence.

Factors That Do Not Matter

With the exception of poverty, most demographic and social characteristics of men and women documented in survey research are not associated with increased risk of intimate partner violence. Age, for example, has occasionally been noted to be a risk factor for such violence, with a greater risk attached to youth, but in most research a relation with age of either partner has not been seen. Similarly, age at marriage is not an associated factor.

Intimate partner violence is mainly a feature of sexual relationships or thwarted sexual relationships in the case of stalking violence. Its relation with marital status varies between settings and is at least partly dependent on the extent to which women have premarital and extramarital sexual relationships. In countries such as Nicaragua where such sexual relationships are rare, intimate partner violence is closely linked to marriage. Where premarital sex is the norm, marital status is not associated with violence. In North America there is a high prevalence of violent experiences in separated or divorced women, but this has not been noted in other countries.

Most household characteristics are not associated with intimate partner violence. These characteristics include living in large or crowded homes and living with in-laws. Similarly, urban or rural residence are not factors. The exception is number of children, which is frequently associated with intimate partner violence. However, in a study in Nicaragua, the first incident in almost all violent relationships occurred within a couple of years of marriage. Thus, rather than a large family causing intimate partner violence, the causation was in the reverse direction.

In North America, belonging to a minority ethnic group has been thought to be associated with intimate partner violence, but associations have been largely explained by differences in education and income. Risk of intimate partner violence varies between countries and between otherwise similar settings within countries. These differences persist after adjustment for social and demographic factors, relationship characteristics, and other risk factors. Some of the differences may be explained by factors such as study design and willingness to disclose violent experience in interview settings. However, other factors also seem to be involved. Research has not been undertaken to identify exactly what these factors are. Possibly they relate to cultural differences in the status of women or acceptability of interpersonal violence. Research aimed at understanding the roots of substantial differences in prevalence between otherwise similar social settings is likely to provide important insights into the causes of violence.

Social Factors Related to Domestic Violence

A commonly held belief in the field of family violence in general, and woman battering in particular, is that violence and abuse cut across all social classes and groups and that anyone can be an abuser. Although there is indeed much empirical support for this conventional wisdom, the data consistently indicate that although abusive behavior cuts across social groups and categories, it *does not do so evenly.* Certain social factors are risk markers of higher rates of violence and battering.

Age   As with all forms of violence and violent criminal behavior, battering is more likely to be committed by men under 30 years of age.

Employment   Unemployed men have higher rates of battering than employed men. Blue-collar workers report higher rates of battering than workers with white-collar occupations.

Income   Given the data on employment and occupation, it is no surprise that men with a low income or who reside in low-income households have higher rates of abusive behavior toward women.

Stress and Marital Conflict   The mechanism through which unemployment, low income, and other factors seem to work to produce battering is likely to be stress. The greater the number of individual, familial, and social stressors individuals encounter, the greater the likelihood of battering behavior. [M.A.] Straus and his colleagues (1980) found a direct relationship between stress and battering only for those men be-

Poverty

Poverty and associated stress are key contributors to intimate partner violence. Although violence occurs in all socioeconomic groups, it is more frequent and severe in lower groups across such diverse settings as the USA, Nicaragua, and India. An influential theory explaining the relation between poverty and intimate partner violence is that it is mediated through stress. Since poverty is inherently stressful, it has been argued that intimate partner violence may result from stress, and that poorer men have fewer resources to reduce stress. However, this finding has not been supported by results from a large study of intimate partner violence in Thailand in which several sources of stress reported by men and their relation with intimate partner violence were analysed.

tween the poverty line and the highest-income group. It seems that those in the top-income group can use economic resources to insulate themselves from the stress of stressor events. For those below the poverty line, the effects of poverty may be so pervasive that additional stressors have little important effect on the likelihood of violent behavior. . . .

Social Isolation . . . It is not entirely clear whether the social isolation is a causal factor or a symptom of a more pervasive pattern of controlling behavior exhibited by the batterer. In other words, isolation might be a causal factor . . . or batterers may deliberately isolate themselves and, more important, their wives or partners, as part of an overall pattern of coercive control.

Alcohol and Drugs The "demon rum" explanation for violence and abuse in the home is one of the most pervasive and widely believed explanations for all forms of violence. Addictive and illicit drugs, such as cocaine, crack, heroin, marijuana, and LSD, are also considered causal agents in child abuse, wife abuse, and other forms of abuse and violence. The relationship among alcohol, drugs, and battering is not [however] as simple as the explanation provided in the "demon rum" mode— that alcohol and other illicit drugs reduce inhibitions and, thus, increase the likelihood of violence.

Michèle Harway and James M. O'Neil, eds., *What Causes Men's Violence Against Women?* Thousand Oaks, CA: Sage Publications, 1999.

Research has shown the importance of levels of conflict in mediating the relation between poverty and abuse. In a study in South Africa, physical violence was not associated in the expected way with indicators of socioeconomic status including ownership of household goods, male and female occupations, and unemployment. Intriguingly, women are protected from intimate partner violence in some of the poorest households, which are those that are mainly supported by someone other than the woman or her partner (43% of all women in the study). Further analysis indicated that this form of extreme poverty reduced the scope for conflicts about household finance.

Financial independence of women is protective in some settings, but not all. Circumstances in which the woman, but not her partner, is working convey additional risk. This finding suggests that economic inequality within a context of poverty is more important than the absolute level of income or empowerment of a man or woman in a relationship. Violence is associated with the product of inequality, whether in the form of advantage to either party. Because socioeconomic injustice at a community or societal level is increasingly being shown to be important in other forms of violence, it might be important in explaining differences in prevalence of intimate partner violence, but there are no data on this factor.

Power and Sex Identity

Within any setting ideas vary on what it means to be a man and what constitutes successful manhood. [R.J.] Gelles first postulated that the link between violence and poverty could be mediated through masculine identity. He argued that men living in poverty were unable to live up to their ideas of "successful" manhood and that, in the resulting climate of stress, they would hit women. Some social scientists have become especially interested in the effect of poverty on male identity and relations between male vulnerability and violence against women. They have argued that such relations are mediated through forms of crisis of masculine identity, which are often infused with ideas about honour and respect.

[P.] Bourgois described how Puerto Rican men growing up in New York slums feel pressurised by models of masculinity and family of their parents' and grandparents' generations, and present-day ideals of successful manhood that emphasise consumerism. Trapped in urban slums, with little or no employment, neither model of masculine success is attainable. In these circumstances, ideals of masculinity are reshaped to emphasise misogyny, substance use, and participation in crime. Violence against women becomes a social norm in which men are violent towards women they can no longer control or economically support. Violence against women is thus seen not just as an expression of male powerfulness and dominance over women, but also as being rooted in male vulnerability stemming from social expectations of manhood that are unattainable because of factors such as poverty experienced by men. Male identity is associated with experiences of power. Challenges to the exercise of power by men can be perceived by them as threats to their masculine identity. An inability to meet social expectations of successful manhood can trigger a crisis of male identity. Violence against women is a means of resolving this crisis because it allows expression of power that is otherwise denied. . . .

Women's Empowerment

High levels of female empowerment seem to be protective against intimate partner violence, but power can be derived from many sources such as education, income, and community roles and not all of these convey equal protection or do so in a direct manner. In many studies, high educational attainment of women was associated with low levels of violence. The same finding has been noted for men. Education confers social empowerment via social networks, self-confidence, and an ability to use information and resources available in society, and may also translate into wealth. The relation between intimate partner violence and female education, however, is complex. In the USA and South Africa the relation has an inverted U-shape, with protection at lowest and highest educational levels.

Cross-cultural research suggests that societies with stronger ideologies of male dominance have more intimate partner violence. These ideologies usually have effects at many levels within a society. At a societal level they affect, for example, female autonomy, access to political systems, influence in the economy, and participation in academic life and the arts. Such ideologies also affect laws, police, criminal justice systems, whether violence against women is criminalised, and the seriousness with which complaints from women about abuse are treated by law enforcers. At an individual level, men who hold conservative ideas about the social status of women are more likely to abuse them. Women who hold more liberal ideas are at greater risk of violence. The degree of liberality of women's ideas on their role and position is closely and positively associated with education—i.e., more educated women are more liberal in these respects. The most likely explanation for the inverted U-shaped relation with education is that having some education empowers women enough to challenge certain aspects of traditional sex roles, but that such empowerment carries an increased risk of violence until a high enough level is reached for protective effects to predominate. Thus, during periods of transition in gender relations women may be at increased risk of violence. . . .

Alcohol

Alcohol consumption is associated with increased risk of all forms of interpersonal violence. Heavy alcohol consumption by men (and often women) is associated with intimate partner violence, if not consistently. Alcohol is thought to reduce inhibitions, cloud judgment, and impair ability to interpret social cues. However, biological links between alcohol and violence are complex. Research on the social anthropology of alcohol drinking suggests that connections between violence and drinking and drunkenness are socially learnt and not universal. Some researchers have noted that alcohol may act as a cultural "time out" for antisocial behaviour. Thus, men are more likely to act violently when drunk because they do not feel they will be held accountable for their behaviour. In some settings, men have described using alcohol in a premeditated manner to enable them to beat their partner because they feel that this is socially expected of them. It seems likely that drugs that reduce inhibition, such as cocaine, will have similar relations to those of alcohol with intimate partner violence, but there has been little population-based research on this subject.

Learned Social Behaviors

Many researchers have discussed intimate partner violence as a learned social behaviour for both men and women. The intergenerational cycling of violence has been documented in many settings. The sons of women who are beaten are more likely to beat their intimate partners and, in some settings, to have been beaten themselves as children. The daughters of women who are beaten are more likely to be beaten as adults. Women who are beaten in childhood by parents are also more likely to be abused by intimate partners as adults. Experiences of violence in the home in childhood teach children that violence is normal in certain settings. In this way, men learn to use violence and women learn to tolerate it or at least tolerate aggressive behaviour.

Cross-cultural studies of intimate partner violence suggest that it is much more frequent in societies where violence is usual in conflict situations and political struggles. An example of this relation is South Africa, where not only is there a history of violent state repression and community insurrection, but also violence is deployed frequently in many situations including disputes between neighbours and colleagues at work. Verbal and physical violence between staff and patients in health settings is also very common and contributes to violence being accepted as a social norm. Many cultures condone the use of physical violence by men against women in certain circumstances and within certain boundaries of severity. In these settings, so long as boundaries are not crossed, the social cost of physical violence is low. This tolerance may result from families or communities emphasising the importance of maintenance of the male-female union at all costs, police trivialising reports of domestic strife, or lack of legislation to protect women.

A Web of Complementary Factors

The causes of intimate partner violence are complex. However, two factors seem to be necessary in an epidemiological sense: the unequal position of women in a particular relationship (and in society) and the normative use of violence in conflict. Without either of these factors, intimate partner violence would not occur. These factors interact with a web of complementary factors to produce intimate partner violence. . . . Violence against women is a demonstration of male power juxtaposed against the lesser power of women. Where women have low status they often lack the necessary perceptions of self-efficacy and the social and economic ability to leave a relationship and return to their family or live alone, and thus are severely curtailed in their ability to act against an abuser. Women might also have no legal access to divorce or redress for abuse. Conversely, at higher levels, empowerment of women protects against violence. Intimate partner violence is increased in settings where the use of violence is normal, and in these settings, sanctions against abusers are often also low. Childhood experiences of violence in the home reinforce for both men and women the normative nature of violence, thus increasing the likelihood of male perpetration and women's acceptance of abuse. Alcohol contributes to intimate partner violence by reducing inhibitions and providing social space for punishment. Similarly, the effects of poverty and economic inequality are mediated through their effect on levels of conflict over resources, women's ability to leave relationships, and men's ability to perceive themselves as successful men.

Periodical Bibliography

The following articles have been selected to supplement the diverse views presented in this chapter.

O.W. Barnett	"Why Battered Women Do Not Leave, Part 1: External Inhibiting Actors Within Society," *Trauma, Violence & Abuse*, October 2000.
Larry Bennett and Oliver J. Williams	"Substance Abuse and Men Who Batter," *Violence Against Women*, May 2003.
Annmarie Cano and Dina Vivian	"Are Life Stressors Associated with Marital Violence?" *Journal of Family Psychology*, September 2003.
W. Fals-Stewart	"The Occurrence of Partner Physical Aggression on Days of Alcohol Consumption: A Longitudinal Diary Study," *Journal of Consulting and Clinical Psychology*, February 2003.
Richard B. Felson and Steven F. Messner	"The Control Motive in Intimate Partner Violence," *Social Psychology Quarterly*, March 2000.
Roland Gustafson	"Male Alcohol-Related Aggression as a Function of Type of Drink," *Aggressive Behavior*, November/December 1999.
Keith McBurnett et al.	"Antisocial Personality, Substance Abuse, and Exposure to Parental Violence in Males Referred for Domestic Violence," *Violence and Victims*, October 2001.
Heather C. Melton and Joanne Belknap	"He Hits, She Hits: Assessing Gender Differences and Similarities in Officially Reported Intimate Partner Violence," *Criminal Justice and Behavior*, June 2003.
Eunice Rodriguez et al.	"The Relation of Family Violence, Employment Status, Welfare Benefits, and Alcohol Drinking in the United States," *Western Journal of Medicine*, May 2001.
Alan Rosenbaum and Penny A. Leisring	"Beyond Power and Control: Towards an Understanding of Partner Abusive Men," *Journal of Comparative Family Studies*, Winter 2003.
Steven P. Swinford et al.	"Harsh Physical Discipline in Childhood and Violence in Later Romantic Involvements: The Mediating Role of Problem Behaviors," *Journal of Marriage and the Family*, May 2000.
Nancy Updike	"Hitting the Wall," *Mother Jones*, May/June 1999.
Chris Wood and Rima Kar	"Why Do Men Do It?: A Recent Spate of Brutal Murders Spurs Debate over Disturbing New Theories About Male Violence," *Maclean's*, August 7, 2000.

CHAPTER 3

Are Legal Remedies Effective in Curbing Domestic Violence?

Chapter Preface

According to a 1996 National Institute of Justice report by Jeffrey Fagan of Columbia University, the legal response to domestic violence has followed three courses: criminal punishment of batterers, treatment programs for batterers, and the issuing of restraining orders to protect victims of abuse. Although many victim advocacy groups have pushed for and monitored the implementation of these legal policies, Fagan is quick to note that there is no consensus on how effective any of these measures are in deterring or stopping domestic violence. As Fagan reports, "For every study that shows promising results, one or more show either no effect or even negative results that increase the risks to victims."

One controversial intervention in domestic violence involves the police response to a disturbance call. All states have instituted domestic violence policy in which police officers on the scene are encouraged to make an arrest if they can determine probable cause (such as seeing a victim's injuries). The prevailing theory is that arresting a suspected batterer ends the immediate threat and allows the victim an opportunity to seek professional services. It also frees the responding officers from any liability of abetting further abuse. Therefore, many states have adopted mandatory arrest laws. UCLA professor Richard A. Berk maintains that these laws, however imperfect, are still the best deterrent to domestic crime because they send a message to batterers that they will be held immediately accountable for their actions.

Critics of mandatory arrest policies argue that giving so much power to law enforcement leaves the victim with little say in the matter. This can keep victims who are in some way dependent on their batterers from reporting any abuse, or it may lead to court cases in which prosecutors are faced with "uncooperative" victims. Some critics also charge that mandatory arrest can prompt batterers to seek revenge on their partners for directly or indirectly involving the police. In addition, as University of Massachusetts professor Eve S. Buzawa and attorney Carl G. Buzawa argue in their 2003 book, *Domestic Violence: The Criminal Justice Response*, arrest may deter a batterer from striking an intimate partner but not from taking those aggressions and lashing out against other victims—children, elderly relatives, or others—who do not seem, to the batterer, to be protected by mandatory arrest laws.

Mandatory arrest laws are just one method law enforcement and the court system use to curb domestic violence. The authors in the following chapter present their views on the effectiveness of other legal intervention strategies.

"Batterers programs as currently configured have modest but positive effects on violence prevention."

Batterer Prevention Programs Are Effective

Larry W. Bennett and Oliver Williams

In the following viewpoint, Larry W. Bennett and Oliver Williams maintain that batterer intervention programs are worthwhile in attempting to curb domestic violence. They examine the success rates of four programs and conclude that while some produced little change in batterers' views of violence, the generally low recidivism rates (the occurrence of subsequent violence) were encouraging. The modest results led the authors to conclude that the type of intervention program employed is not important, but the effects of intervention are nevertheless significant. Larry W. Bennett is an associate professor at the University of Illinois Jane Addams School of Social Work. Oliver Williams is the executive director of the Institute on Domestic Violence in the African American Community and an associate professor in the Graduate School of Social Work at the University of Minnesota in Minneapolis. He has also worked as a counselor in the field of domestic violence for over twenty years.

As you read, consider the following questions:

1. According to Bennett and Williams, what are the three main goals of batterer intervention programs?
2. What is the "stake in conformity" hypothesis, as defined by the authors?

Batterer intervention programs (BIPs) are designed for men arrested for domestic violence and for men who would be arrested if their actions were public. These programs usually consist of educational classes or treatment groups, but may include other intervention elements such as extensive evaluation, individual counseling, or case management. Because 80% of batterers are referred by the criminal justice system, one set of implicit goals for BIPs includes justice and accountability, goals that have not been adequately recognized in evaluations of BIPs. Another goal of BIPs is victim safety. Most standards for BIPs specify that service providers consider victim safety implications when implementing interventions such as contacting victims for information about the batterer. A final goal for BIPs is rehabilitation and behavioral changes such as skill building, attitude change, and emotional development.

The details of conducting batterer intervention programs are readily available. The purpose of this paper is to look not at what batterer programs do, but rather at the effectiveness of these programs. Knowledge about batterer program effectiveness is important for several reasons.

Increasingly, courts are referring men convicted of domestic abuse to batterers intervention programs, suggesting a certain level of public confidence in the effectiveness of these programs. Is that confidence justified? Second, victims of domestic violence often want to remain in a relationship with their partner and are looking for help in changing his violent and controlling behavior. Since a batterer seeking counseling is one of the strongest predictors that a woman will return to her batterer, advocates are justifiably concerned that batterer programs not hold out a promise of hope which may become a vehicle for injury. Third, people who work with batterers are interested in outcomes so they can improve the level of program effectiveness; for these people, the concern is less *whether* batterer programs work, but *how* they work, *for whom* do they work best, and *which elements* of the program are most important. . . .

Overall Evaluations

The main questions to be addressed are: (1) Are batterer intervention programs effective when compared to customary practice (usually probation)? and (2) Are certain approaches to batterer intervention programming more effective than other approaches? Our conclusions will be these: (1) Batterers programs as currently configured have modest but positive effects on violence prevention, and (2) there is little evidence at present supporting the effectiveness of one BIP approach over another.

Table 1 summarizes the four experimental studies from which we can best draw conclusions about the first question: are batterer intervention programs effective when compared to customary practice? . . .

As we see in Table 1, two of the four experiments (Dunford, 2000; Feder & Forde, 2000) found no difference in recidivism for men in the batterer program and men in the control condition. The other two experiments (Palmer et al., 1992; Taylor, Davis & Maxwell, 2001) found small but significant reductions in recidivism for men in batterer programs. While it is beyond the scope of this paper to provide a detailed analysis of these experiments, they make such an important contribution to our understanding of batterers programs that they merit the short descriptions that follow.

Ontario Experiment

The first experiment comparing batterer programs to a control group was conducted by Palmer and her colleagues in Hamilton, Ontario. [S.E.] Palmer, [R.A.] Brown, and [M.E.] Barrera (1992) studied 59 men convicted of wife abuse, placed on probation, and randomly assigned to either a 10-week batterer program at a local family service agency, or to probation with no batterer program. The intervention was characterized by the researchers as psycho-educational and client-centered. Seventy percent of the BIP participants completed their program, and 87% attended at least half the sessions. A year after the program ended, all subjects and partners were mailed questionnaires followed by phone calls, but the response rate was low. Police records were searched for complaints or arrests. Three of the 30 (10%) men assigned to the batterer program re-offended, according to police records, compared to eight of 26 (31%) men receiving probation only. Most criticism of this study focuses on the small number of participants. . . .

Table 1: Summary of Batterer Programs Evaluations Random Assignment to Control Group Designs

Experiment	BIP	Sample Size	Recidivism	
			By Victim Report	By Official Report
Ontario (Palmer et al., 1992)	10-week, 1.5 hour psycho-education group	Probation	56	N/A	BIP 10, Control 31
San Diego Navy (Dunford, 2000)	12 months, cognitive-behavioral therapy group	Safety planning	309	BIP 29, Control 35	BIP 4, Control 4
Broward County (Feder & Forde, 2000)	Probation + 6 months of Duluth model group	Probation	404	N/A	BIP 4, Control 5
Brooklyn (Taylor et al., 2001)	40-hour Duluth model group	40 hours of community service	376	BIP 22, Control 15	BIP 16, Control 26
			Average	BIP 26	BIP 9
			Recidivism	Control 25	Control 17

Navy Experiment

[F.W.] Dunford (2000) reports the results of an experiment at the Navy base in San Diego where 861 men who assaulted their wives were randomly assigned to one of four conditions: (a) six months of weekly cognitive-behavioral treatment, followed by six months of monthly groups; (b) six months of group for couples, followed by six months of monthly group; (c) a rigorous monitoring and case management program similar to probation, or (d) safety planning, similar to the work of victim advocates, which serves as a control group. Seventy percent of the men completed their program. In Table 1, we consider only (a) the BIP and (d) the control group. Standard practice in batterer intervention excludes groups for couples as a threat to victim safety, and in fact, two thirds of the female members of the couples in (b) were not present during the couples group, possibly voting with their feet on the popularity among victims of the couples' model. Dunford found no significant differences between the four groups. Were the experiment generalizable to other batterers programs, we would conclude that batterers programs had no significant effect on domestic abuse. . . . The overall recidivism rate was 30% by spouse report and 4% by arrest. These figures compare very favorably with other interventions. What we can conclude from the Navy experiment is this: If communities take a proactive response to domestic violence, including assertive probation work, sanctions for non-compliance, victim safety monitoring, and batterer intervention programs, they will probably reduce the incidence of repeat violence.

Broward Experiment

[L.] Feder and [D.R.] Forde (2000) studied all 404 male defendants convicted of misdemeanor domestic violence in Broward County Florida (Fort Lauderdale) over a five month period. Men were randomly assigned to either probation and six months of a Duluth model BIP[1] or probation only. Researchers collected information on minor and severe abuse, violations of probation and re-arrests using offender self-reports, victim reports, and official measures. Ninety-five percent of the men assigned to the BIP attended at least 20 of 26 meetings, a rather remarkable figure when compared to the average BIP attrition rate of 50%. Since less than a third of victims could be interviewed at follow-up, these results are not included in Table 1. At 12-month follow-up, there were no differences between the BIP participants and regular probationers on measures of attitude toward women, beliefs about wife-beating, attitudes toward treating domestic violence as a crime, beliefs about the female partner's responsibility for the violence, estimated chance of hitting partner in the next year, and victim or official report of recidivism. One of the key findings of the Broward experiment was further support for the *stake in conformity* hypothesis: men most likely to re-offend are those who have the least to lose, as measured by education, marital status, home ownership, employment, income, and length of residency. This finding is robust over

---

1. The Duluth model assumes batterers wish to control their partners. The program, therefore, relies on batterers' confronting this desire and learning behaviors to change it.

a number of BIP studies and presents one of the most formidable obstacles to effective batterer intervention programs, as well as evaluating those programs.

Brooklyn Experiment

[B.G.] Taylor, [R.C.] Davis, and [C.D.] Maxwell (2001) report the findings of 376 men convicted of misdemeanor domestic violence and randomly assigned to 40 hours of a Duluth model BIP or 40 hours of community service. Victim reports and official records were used to track differences at six-month and 12-month follow-up. At follow-up with partners, BIP participants were more likely than controls to have been abusive, but the difference was not significant. Using criminal justice records, BIP participants were 50% less likely to have re-offended at both six-month and 12-month follow-ups. However, enthusiasm for this result is tempered by the fact that judge, prosecutor, and defendant had to agree on the man's referral to the BIP, a process which effectively screened out men with low motivation.

Small but Important Contribution

Considering these four experiments, along with a growing body of quasi-experimental and non-experimental studies, we conclude that the effect of BIPs is modest, but nevertheless significant. By significant, we do not necessarily mean statistically significant, but rather practically significant. Asking whether batterers programs are more effective than probation alone is asking the wrong question because batterer programs were never designed to be used instead of probation. Augmenting the influence of probation and providing an additional vehicle for accountability is one of the goals of batterer programs. If there were no statistically positive effects for batterers programs, which is clearly not the case according to the research, then we could rightly say these programs were not effective. The best statement we can make at this time is that BIPs add a small but important effect to overall violence prevention.

"The Broward County [Florida] study found that the batterer intervention program had little or no effect."

Batterer Prevention Programs May Be Ineffective

National Institute of Justice

Batterer intervention programs are alternatives to incarceration and are designed to convince batterers to adopt nonviolent strategies to deal with domestic disputes. In the following report by the National Institute of Justice (NIJ), a branch of the U.S. Department of Justice, two batterer intervention programs working with male offenders were measured for their success rates. Men completing the two programs—one in Broward County, Florida, and the other in Brooklyn, New York—showed little change in their attitudes toward violence and a fairly high rearrest rate for subsequent assault.

As you read, consider the following questions:

1. According to this NIJ report, which of the two intervention programs had a marked effect on their subjects' attitudes toward domestic abuse?
2. In the Broward County program, what percentage of the attendees were rearrested at least once after the program was completed? How does that compare to the rearrest percentage for the control group that did not attend the program?
3. What are some of the evaluation improvements the NIJ report recommends?

National Institute of Justice, "Do Batterer Intervention Programs Work? Two Studies," *National Institute of Justice Report*, September 2003.

Batterer intervention programs have been proliferating in the United States for the past two decades. These programs give batterers an alternative to jail. They usually involve several months of attendance at group therapy sessions that attempt to stop the violence and change the batterers' attitudes toward women and battering.

Programs Might Be Ineffective

Two recent evaluations, one in Broward County, Florida, and the other in Brooklyn, New York, evaluated interventions based on the Duluth model, which is the most commonly used program in the Nation. Many States mandate its use. The Broward County study found that the batterer intervention program had little or no effect, and the Brooklyn study found only minor improvement in some subjects. Neither program changed subjects' attitudes toward domestic abuse.

However, limitations in the studies raise additional issues. Are the evaluations correct that these programs don't change batterers' behavior and attitudes, or do shortcomings in the evaluations cover up program effects? There is no adequate answer to this question. Both issues may need to be addressed in future programs and studies.

Does Stake-in-Conformity Matter Most?

The Broward County study found no significant difference between the treatment and control groups in attitudes toward the role of women, whether wife beating should be a crime, or whether the State has the right to intervene in cases of domestic violence. It also found no significant difference between these groups in whether victims expected their partners to beat them again. Moreover, no significant difference was found in violations of probation or rearrests, except that men who were assigned to the program but did not attend all sessions were more likely to be rearrested than members of the control group.

Evaluators tried to determine what could account for differences in men's self-reports of physical violence. They considered whether the offender was assigned to treatment; the number of classes he attended; and such stake-in-conformity variables as marital status, residential stability, and employment. These last factors proved crucial.

Attending the program had no effect on the incidence of physical violence. Rather, offenders who were employed, married, and/or owned a home were less likely to batter again. Younger men and men with no stable residence (regardless of age) were more likely to abuse their partners. Older men who owned a home were less likely to do so.

Twenty-four percent of men in both the experimental and control groups were rearrested at least once during their year on probation. Again, attending the program had no effect. Rather, whether an offender was employed (a stake-in-conformity variable) seemed to have more influence on whether he was rearrested.

Is Longer Treatment More Effective?

The Brooklyn study unintentionally had two experimental groups of offenders. After the study was under-way, defense attorneys objected to the 26-week program's duration and cost and advised their clients not to participate. To preserve the study, offenders were offered an accelerated 8-week program, which created a second experimental sample.

Batterers assigned to 26 weeks of treatment were less likely than the control group and those assigned to 8-week classes to be arrested again for a crime against the same victim. Neither program changed batterers' attitudes toward domestic violence. There were significant differences in reoffending, however. Even though more offenders completed the shorter program, the 26-week group had fewer criminal complaints than either the control group or the 8-week group.

Men who attended the longer treatment committed fewer new violent acts than those who attended the shorter treatment or those who had no treatment. This may suggest that providing treatment for a longer period of time helped reduce battering during the term of treatment and for some time thereafter.

Evaluation Issues

Concerns about research methodology cloud most batterer intervention program evaluations, and these two studies were no exception. The major issues are

- Maintaining sample integrity. Keeping assignments to batterer programs truly random is consistently a challenge.
- Low attendance, high attrition, difficulty following up. High dropout and low response rates can lead to overly positive estimates of program effects.
- Inadequate data sources. Official records used to validate batterer and victim reports may be collected inconsistently across jurisdictions; also, they capture only those violations that reach the authorities. Evidence suggests that batterers often avoid rearrest by switching to psychological and verbal abuse.
- Difficulty measuring outcomes. Evaluators lack good survey instruments to measure batterer behavior and attitudes. The revised Conflict Tactics Scale (CTS2) [a system used to rank the severity of aggressive behavior] used in these studies was not designed for before and after measurements. The Brooklyn study raised another issue common to batterer intervention program studies: Do evaluations examine the effects of the intervention or the effects of assignment to a treatment group?
- Who is defining success? A final concern is broader in scope: Is a mere reduction in violence enough? These studies considered a reduction in violence to be a success based on the premise that it is unrealistic to expect batterers to abandon violent behavior after one intervention. But a "statistically significant reduction in violence" may mean little to a battered woman.

A New Approach

The bottom line is: What are the best ways to protect victims? Batterer intervention programs are one approach, although much remains to be learned about them, specifically, which program works best for which batterer under which circumstances. But perhaps what is needed is a whole new approach.

Rethinking intervention. The models that underlie batterer intervention programs may need improvement. New approaches based on research into the causes of battering and batterer profiles may be more productive than a one-size-fits-all approach. Researchers may also draw lessons from other disciplines, such as substance abuse interventions for example, that length of treatment may influence the outcome.

Types of Batterer Interventions

The Broward County and Brooklyn batterer intervention programs were based on the Duluth model. The Duluth model's underlying theory is that batterers want to control their partners and that changing this dynamic is key to changing their behavior. Its curriculum uses a "power and control wheel" depicting tactics abusers use to control their partners. Themes counteracting these tactics are discussed in classes and group sessions that attempt to induce batterers to confront their attitudes and behavior.

There are several alternatives to the Duluth model. Cognitive-behavioral intervention views battering as a result of errors in thinking and focuses on skills training and anger management. Another model, group practice, works from the premise that battering has multiple causes and is best addressed through a combined approach that includes an individual needs assessment. Proponents of these programs believe that a more long-term approach than the Duluth model is necessary.

Programs based on batterer typologies or profiles are gaining popularity. These interventions profile the batterer through a psychological assessment, then classify him by level of risk, substance abuse, and other factors that may influence which intervention is most likely to work for him. Programs based on this approach are still relatively new and not fully evaluated.

A controversial intervention is couples therapy, which views men and women as equally responsible for creating disturbances in the relationship. It is widely criticized for assigning the victim a share of the blame for the continuation of violence.

National Institute of Justice, September 2003.

Improvements in how programs are put into practice may also be necessary, since variations in how programs are carried out may reduce their effectiveness. Researchers have noted greater effects in demonstration programs implemented by researchers than in practical programs implemented by juvenile or criminal justice agencies. Thus, the degree to which a program is faithful to the intervention model may determine how well it works. For example, some programs have few sanctions for dropping out, whereas others closely monitor attendance. This suggests the need to test the effectiveness of close monitoring and required attendance.

Linking batterer programs to other programs and responses. Batterer intervention programs may be effective only in the context of a broader criminal justice and community response to domestic violence that includes arrest, restraining orders, intensive monitoring of batterers, and changes to social norms that inadvertently tolerate partner violence.

If monitoring is partly responsible for lower reoffense rates, as the Brooklyn experiment suggests, judicial monitoring may be a useful approach. The Judicial Oversight Demonstration initiative, a collaboration among the National Institute of Justice, the Office on Violence Against Women, and three local jurisdictions, is testing this idea. Other innovations might include mandatory intervention (indeterminate probation) until the batterer no longer endangers his partner, an approach that has been used with sex offenders.

Better Evaluation

Improving evaluations. Although the quality of batterer intervention program evaluations has improved, barriers remain. By collaborating, researchers, practitioners, and policymakers may be able to develop better strategies and improve the rigor of experimental evaluations.

For example, researchers need to find better ways to maintain contact with batterers and victims and better instruments than the revised CTS2. They need to develop more reliable ways of validating batterer and victim reports than relying strictly on official records of rearrests and probation violations. Statistical tools can be applied to correct for nonrandom assignment and other problems.

Since batterer intervention programs are a relatively new response to a critical social problem, it is too early to abandon the concept. More work needs to be done to determine the causes of battering and test new responses.

"Without question, mandatory reporting has improved the identification and treatment of those suffering from domestic violence."

Mandatory Reporting Is Effective

Hillary Larkin and Nancy O'Malley

In 1994, California signed into law a bill that required health-care workers to report any patient injuries caused or suspected to be caused by domestic violence. All health-care providers must immediately make this information known to police, thus freeing themselves of criminal liability. Several other states joined California in passing similar mandatory reporting laws. Hillary Larkin and Nancy O'Malley argue, in the following viewpoint, that mandatory reporting laws are a necessary part of the legal remedy to domestic violence. By reporting abuse, health-care workers take the first steps in bringing help to victims who might be too afraid to ask for it. Hillary Larkin works in the emergency department at the Alameda County Medical Center in Oakland, California. Nancy O'Malley works at the Alameda County District Attorney's Office in Oakland.

As you read, consider the following questions:

1. According to Larkin and O'Malley, what message does the California mandatory reporting law send to abusers?
2. In the authors' opinion, how does the California law uphold patient autonomy?
3. How does the California law protect health-care workers, according to the authors?

Heidi M. Bauer et al., "California's Mandatory Reporting of Domestic Violence Injuries: Does the Law Go Too Far or Not Far Enough?" *Western Journal of Medicine*, August 1999. Copyright © 1999 by the *Western Journal of Medicine*. Reproduced by permission.

It wasn't long ago that when the police responded to a domestic violence call, one officer would take the batterer around the block to "walk it off" while another officer stayed with the victim to "calm her down." Thankfully, that procedure has changed.

It wasn't long ago that if the victim of domestic violence told the police or district attorney that she did not want to "press charges," the matter was quickly dismissed. Nowadays most, if not all, prosecuting attorneys' offices have adopted a "no-drop" policy, which means that every case of domestic violence will be pursued if legally possible.

It took many years of advocacy and perseverance to change the way in which law enforcement officials respond to domestic violence. Healthcare providers should be held to the same standard. California's legislation that requires healthcare providers to report domestic violence injuries has successfully improved the response of the healthcare system to domestic violence, enabling the criminal justice system to enforce the law better.

As Institutions Respond, Professional Training Increases

Since the mandatory reporting legislation was enacted, we have seen a dramatic increase in the commitment made by healthcare institutions to address domestic violence. A few years ago, only 54% of emergency departments in California reported having policies and protocols for managing victims of domestic violence. Today they often have standardized injury forms, information packets for patients, cameras for documenting injuries, and social service workers poised to intervene. We also have seen greater cooperation among healthcare institutions, law enforcement agencies, social services, and domestic violence advocates.

Mandatory reporting requirements have also increased professional training and continuing education on domestic violence issues. Because healthcare providers are now legally liable for reporting, they are motivated to acquire greater knowledge and skills. This training increases knowledge, comfort, skills for effective inquiry and intervention, and even screening practices. The demands, finding, and resources for these domestic violence programs would likely disappear if mandatory reporting by healthcare providers were repealed.

Better Identification, Treatment, and Documentation

Without question, mandatory reporting has improved the identification and treatment of those suffering from domestic violence. Even those patients who present vague stories are now encountering healthcare providers who are familiar with the "red flags" of domestic violence. Trained healthcare providers can demonstrate concern, ask critical questions, and create an environment where patients feel safe. They can communicate to victims that domestic violence is no longer considered simply a "family matter," so they will not be judged for being in such a relationship.

Mandatory reporting potentially improves documentation of domestic violence for use in criminal prosecution, divorce, child custody, and civil cases. Medical records and, less commonly, physician testimony have long been used in both civil and criminal cases as evidence of a history of domestic violence. California's mandatory reporting law strengthens this tradition by requiring healthcare providers to be specific about the cause of injury and the name of the perpetrator. In addition, the statute recommends that providers improve medical recordkeeping by including a body map of the injuries and information about past domestic violence.

Holding the Perpetrator Responsible

Mandatory reporting sends a clear message to the victim and to society that domestic violence is a crime and will not be tolerated. It is essential that our law enforcement agencies hold the batterer accountable, through incarceration or court-ordered counseling. The strongest deterrent to continued violence is the threat of incarceration, and prosecuting attorneys in California are able to convict batterers without the cooperation or participation of the victim. Failing to report domestic violence injuries is tantamount to aiding and abetting a batterer and deprives the victim of the opportunity for the criminal justice system to work.

Although opponents to the law suggest that reporting to police may cause retaliation by the batterer, we believe that the violence is more likely to escalate in the absence of intervention. The healthcare provider's report to police provides an opportunity for intervention, which may be the only hope of stopping the violence. Domestic violence is a prelude to murder. For many victims, it is only a matter of time. Mandatory reporting by healthcare providers gives victims and their children a chance at survival in an environment free of violence.

Upholding Patient Autonomy

Under the California law, patients do not retain the right to refuse reporting. They do retain the right to refuse to interact with the police or social service providers, and thus their fundamental autonomy is upheld. Ten years ago, mandatory reporting of sexual assault crimes was harshly criticized for its paternalism. Interestingly, it is now widely accepted that sexual assault is a serious crime warranting law enforcement involvement, no matter what the circumstances of the victim or the relationship with the sex offender. Much like domestic violence, the victims of sexual assault are typically competent adults who have experienced a violent crime, often at the hands of someone known to them.

Often, through emotional support and honest discussions, patients can be persuaded to cooperate with law enforcement. These discussions provide an opportunity to educate victims about the risks to themselves and their children, their legal options, and opportunities for shelter and support in their community. Although victims may want to avoid family disruption, they need to understand that the violence and abuse are not in their family's best interest. In fact, these discussions can help many victims find the resolve to leave their abusive partners in order to protect their children. Patient education shifts the responsibility for the violence from the victim to the batterer.

Protecting Providers from Liability

Among healthcare providers, before the legislation was enacted, ambiguity existed about reporting domestic violence. This ambiguity created conflict and fear and left healthcare workers wondering if they had done the right thing. Today, the mandatory reporting law gives healthcare providers protection from liability, as well as clear directions on how to proceed with a patient.

There will always be room for individual judgment, but healthcare providers need to bear in mind their obligations to avoid causing harm, to prevent serious injury, and to act for the benefit of the patient. Consider the case of the emergency department practitioner who treated a domestic violence victim. Despite police and social service efforts, the patient was gunned down by her batterer the following morning. As the practitioner so poignantly stated, "I recognized the signs, I was able to get her to tell her story. I know that I did everything, along with the police and the advocate, to try to help her. I can't imagine how I would feel if I had done nothing."

Some healthcare providers may feel that reporting will

not stop the violence or protect the victim. They should recognize that this sentiment is an institutional form of learned helplessness. We have the capability to make a positive impact on the victims of violence every day. We need to work together to combat the feeling of institutional helplessness. As professionals, we all have a role to play in protecting victims of domestic violence and holding our colleagues accountable to sharing the commitment to stop domestic violence. For healthcare providers, mandatory reporting is the first step to forming collaborations with other professionals who assist victims of domestic violence. If a healthcare provider were driving home from work and saw a domestic violence assault in progress, one would hope he or she would call the police. Should it be any different in the workplace?

"Clinician reporting to police . . . may lead some abused patients to avoid seeking help from health care clinicians."

Mandatory Reporting Should Be Reconsidered

Michael A. Rodriguez, Elizabeth McLoughlin, Gregory Nah, and Jacquelyn C. Campbell

In some states, medical professionals are required to report any confirmed or suspected domestic abuse injuries to authorities. In the following article, Michael A. Rodriguez and colleagues report the results of a survey of emergency room patients on this issue. According to their findings, nearly half of the abused women surveyed were opposed to mandatory reporting. Among these, the majority were in favor of mandatory reporting only with the patient's consent. The results prompted the authors to recommend that mandatory reporting laws be amended to take the patient's preference into consideration. Michael A. Rodriguez is an M.D. affiliated with the Department of Family and Community Medicine at the University of California, San Francisco. Elizabeth McLoughlin and Gregory Nah are members of the Trauma Foundation. Jacquelyn C. Campbell is part of the Johns Hopkins University School of Nursing.

As you read, consider the following questions:
1. In California, what penalties do clinicians face if they fail to report evidence of domestic violence?
2. According to the authors' survey, what percentage of abused women opposed mandatory reporting?

Michael A. Rodriguez, Elizabeth McLoughlin, Gregory Nah, and Jacquelyn C. Campbell, "Mandatory Reporting of Domestic Violence Injuries to the Police: What Do Emergency Department Patients Think?" *JAMA: The Journal of the American Medical Association*, August 1, 2001. Copyright © 2001 by the American Medical Association. Reproduced by permission.

M ost states require clinicians to report to police injuries due to violence, criminal acts, or deadly weapons. From 1991 to 1994, California, Colorado, Rhode Island, and Kentucky passed various forms of mandatory reporting laws requiring health care professionals to report intimate partner violence (IPV) to the police. Since 1994, California has required clinicians to report to police suspected IPV-related injuries, even if this is contrary to patient wishes. Noncomplying clinicians face penalties of fines up to $1000 and/or jail sentences of up to 6 months in California. The law does not specify how police should respond, local jurisdictions vary in response, and the degree of enforcement is unknown.

What Opponents Fear

Mandatory reporting is controversial among clinicians, patients, and domestic violence prevention advocates. Supporters of the policy argue that it will facilitate the prosecution of batterers, encourage health care clinicians to identify domestic violence, and improve data collection. Opponents believe it may increase violence by the perpetrators, diminish patients' autonomy, and compromise patient-clinician confidentiality. Mandatory reporting laws are not affected by the new Federal Medical Privacy Protections for Victims of Domestic Violence because they fall under the provision relating to disclosures required by law. The National Resource Council has recommended a moratorium on such laws until more research is conducted on the advantages and disadvantages of mandatory reporting policies for domestic violence.

While patients frequently look to police for help during acute episodes of violence, clinician reporting to police may raise fears of increased violence, loss of control, and family separation, all of which may lead some abused patients to avoid seeking help from health care clinicians. Two recent studies have found that some women may be supportive of mandatory reporting policies. However, another study reports that a majority of abused patients are opposed to mandatory reporting of IPV to police. A Colorado study found that 9% of female patient respondents were less likely to seek medical care as a result of mandatory reporting. Limitations of these studies include low response rates, small sample sizes, or samples primarily from states where specific domestic violence mandatory reporting laws do not exist. An evaluation of an emergency department intervention to improve the health system response to abused patients permitted us to survey a large random sample of female patients in California and Pennsylvania about mandatory reporting. Unlike California, Pennsylvania does not have a specific law that mandates clinicians to report IPV to police.

The Survey

The patient survey was part of an emergency department IPV intervention study and involved 12 emergency departments, randomly drawn from all midsized hospitals (20000–40000 patient visits annually) within 160 km of San Francisco, Calif, and Pittsburgh, Pa. In contrast to previous published analyses of 3 waves of data collection for 11 of these 12 emergency departments, this study used only the third wave of patient surveys from all 12 emergency departments. Response rates had improved for that wave and the questions on mandatory reporting had been revised to allow for better assessment of patient preferences. We attempted to survey 1672 patients during 1996 using the Patient Satisfaction and Safety Survey, an anonymous self-administered questionnaire. The questionnaire contained 20 items designed to (1) verify eligibility for participation; (2) identify patients currently in abusive relationships; (3) assess satisfaction with care; and (4) determine attitudes about mandatory reporting of domestic violence to police. To assess abuse status and identify those patients with histories of physical or sexual partner violence in the previous year we used the Abuse Assessment Screen. To assess patients' attitudes toward the mandatory reporting law, respondents were asked the question: "Do you think that the emergency department staff in hospitals should be required to call the police when they think that a husband, boyfriend, or partner (ex-husband, ex-boyfriend, ex-partner) has hurt or abused an adult patient?" Respondents were given 3 options: (1) yes, every time; (2) every time unless the patient objects; or (3) never. . . .

A total of 1218 eligible emergency department patients responded to the Patient Satisfaction and Safety Survey (response rate, 72.8%). Overall, the response rates for respondents who answered the question on mandatory reporting and completed information on each characteristic ranged from 67.3% to 70.2%. There were no significant state-specific differences in response to the survey attitudinal questions, including support for or opposition to mandatory reporting laws. Overall, 12.0% of respondents (n=140) reported being physically abused or forced to have sexual activities in the previous year.

Results of a Survey of Physicians

Overall, an estimated 59% of California primary care and emergency physicians reported that they might not comply with the reporting law if a patient objected. Reported noncompliance with the mandatory reporting law varied significantly among the medical specialties depending on whether a patient objected. Compared with emergency physicians, primary care providers reported significantly higher rates of noncompliance when a patient objected. . . .

Other factors associated with noncompliance included prior knowledge of the law, a recent course on domestic violence, and practice type. Self-reported noncompliance did not differ by sex, age, ethnicity, country of training, or having identified an abuse victim in a clinical setting. . . . Lack of prior awareness of the law also increased noncompliance.

Michael A. Rodriguez et al., "Mandatory Reporting of Intimate Partner Violence to Police: Views of Physicians in California," *American Journal of Public Health*, April 1999.

Among the abused respondents, 44.3% (n=62) opposed mandatory reporting of domestic violence to police. (36.4% (n=51) supported reporting but only with patient consent; 7.9% (n=11) thought that physicians should never report to police), while 55.7% (n=78) supported mandatory reporting. Of nonabused respondents 70.7% (n=728) reported higher levels of support for the policy, while 29.3% (n=301) opposed the law (25.7% [n=264] favored reporting with consent; 3.6% [n=37]) preferred physicians never to report).

Women who opposed the mandatory reporting policy tended to be young (34.3% of 18–39 years old vs 28.3% of those [greater than] 40 years old); nonwhite (35.9% of nonwhite patients vs 29.0% of white patients); non-English speakers at home (41.7% of non-English speakers vs 30.3% of primary English speakers); and abused (44.3% of those reporting abuse in the past year vs 29.2% of those reporting no abuse). Opposition to the policy did not differ significantly by relationship status, total family income per month, or state (California vs Pennsylvania). . . .

The Desire for Patient Consent

In this study, 44.3% of recently abused female emergency department patients do not support mandatory reporting of domestic violence to police. Possible reasons for such opposition include fear of retaliation by the abuser, fear of family separation, mistrust of the legal system, and preference for confidentiality and autonomy in the patient-clinician relationship. Yet, our study also demonstrated that a higher percentage (55.7%) of recently abused female emergency department patients do support mandatory reporting. This may be due to desires for enhanced safety and relief from the onus of making a police report.

Many patients supported IPV reporting policies that take into consideration patients' preferences. For example, of the 44.3% of women with recent histories of abuse who opposed mandatory reporting, the very women who would potentially be reported to police, the majority selected the response indicating support for reporting to police unless the patient objects. Further research with abused women is needed to distinguish their preferences among several options: (1) a law requiring reporting unless the patient objects; (2) a reporting law that requires patient consent; or (3) no reporting laws but physician responsiveness to IPV and assistance with criminal justice interventions when desired.

Similar to the women with recent histories of abuse, 41.7% of women who were primarily non-English speakers were opposed to mandatory reporting. These findings are consistent with previous qualitative research in which abused women expressed the belief that they should control the decisions to involve the police. Another study has explored sociopolitical factors that hinder abused immigrant women from seeking help, including social isolation, language barriers, and fear of deportation. Because the impact of police involvement in immigrant women's lives may be different than for US-born women, changes in welfare and immigration laws may interact with this policy, resulting in further disempowerment of the female patient. Given the attitudes expressed by the respondents in these studies, it is unclear whether mandatory reporting will help recent IPV survivors or put them at risk for further violence. One clinical alternative is to encourage the assessment of danger that can help women and clinicians assess safety, yet leave the final decision as to whether to call the police with the patient.

Physicians' attitudes regarding mandatory reporting have varied. In a previous survey of physicians in California, 53% to 85% responded that such policies could prevent women from seeking medical care, provoke retaliation, or compromise confidentiality and autonomy. In the same survey, 53% to 86% believed that these policies can increase recognition and responsiveness to domestic violence, as well as improve and increase documentation and collection of statistics.

One limitation of our study is that we only surveyed patients seeking care at emergency departments. Therefore, we missed IPV survivors who may have been deterred from seeking help for reasons that include fear that they may be reported to the police. This limitation would have the impact of underestimating the degree of opposition among abused women to laws that mandate reporting IPV to police.

Further research on mandatory reporting is needed to address the preferences of those in abusive relationships. Research should also track patient and clinician outcomes in other states that require reporting IPV to police. Lacking answers to these concerns, our research suggests that policymakers should consider development of IPV reporting policy options that combine respect for patient autonomy with the greatest potential for protection from abuse.

Periodical Bibliography

The following articles have been selected to supplement the diverse views presented in this chapter.

Ileana Arias et al.	"Violence Against Women: The State of Batterer Prevention Programs," *Journal of Law, Medicine & Ethics*, Fall 2002.
Larry W. Bennett	"In Defense of Batterer-Program Standards," *Families in Society*, January/February 1998.
Fran S. Danis	"The Criminalization of Domestic Violence: What Social Workers Need to Know," *Social Work*, April 2003.
Rebecca Emerson Dobash	"Domestic Violence: Arrest, Prosecution, and Reducing Violence," *Criminology & Public Policy*, March 2003.
Laura Dugan	"Domestic Violence Legislation: Exploring Its Impact on the Likelihood of Domestic Violence, Police Involvement, and Arrest," *Criminology & Public Policy*, March 2003.
Edward W. Gondolf and Alison Snow Jones	"The Program Effect of Batterer Programs in Three Cities," *Violence and Victims*, December 2001.
James Lasley	"The Effect of Intensive Bail Supervision on Repeat Domestic Violence Offenders," *Policy Studies Journal*, May 2003.
Tom Lininger	"A Better Way to Disarm Batterers," *Hastings Law Journal*, March 2003.
Judith McFarlane et al.	"Women Filing Assault Charges on an Intimate Partner: Criminal Justice Outcome and Future Violence Experienced," *Violence Against Women*, April 2000.
Rhonda McMillion	"Stronger Voice for Victims; Reauthorized Violence Against Women Act Expands Scope of Programs," *ABA Journal*, December 2000.
Jon Naito	"Protection Orders Do Help, Study Finds 80% Reduction in Violence Against Women Reported in Seattle Analysis," *Seattle Post-Intelligencer*, August 7, 2002.
Glenn Sacks	"California NOW's Family Court Report 2002: Faulty Research, False Conclusions," *Los Angeles Daily Journal*, July 11, 2002.
Alisa Smith	"It's My Decision, Isn't It? A Research Note on Battered Women's Perceptions of Mandatory Intervention Laws," *Violence Against Women*, December 2000.
Leslie M. Tutty et al.	"An Evaluation of Men's Batterer Treatment Groups," *Research on Social Work Practice*, November 2001.

CHAPTER 4

How Can Social Services Reduce Domestic Violence?

Chapter Preface

Community support groups for abused women began in the 1970s as extensions of women's shelters. Women seeking refuge from abusive partners were offered information on abuse and the services that could help them further. From the shelter system, support groups became a mainstay of a variety of women's advocacy groups that sprang up as more and more attention was focused on domestic violence. Since some of these groups are no longer tied to shelters, they include women who are still in abusive relationships as well as those that have left them.

Support groups typically meet in weekly sessions and are led by professional counselors or women who have lived through abusive relationships. The group setting allows women to express their own concerns, share personal accounts, and learn about other available services. According to an article on support groups written by Leslie M. Tutty and Michael Rothery for the *Handbook of Domestic Violence Intervention Strategies* (2003), the rhetoric of the counselors is generally informed by the same guidelines proposed by many experts who write on domestic violence treatment. Tutty and Rothery state, "Most authors recommend that those who work with battered women adopt a feminist belief system that condemns violence, avoids assigning responsibility for the violence to victims, recognizes how social institutions perpetuate violence, and focuses on violence rather than the couples' interactions." The goal is to rebuild the victims' self-esteem, get them to recognize that they are not isolated, and help them understand that violence should have no part in any relationship.

Although the objectives seem admirable, some women contend that, in practice, support groups send a very different message. In a 2003 article for iFeminists.com, Nev Moore relates her experiences after being remanded to a support group by the Massachusetts Department of Social Services (DSS). "I found it repulsive," Moore writes, "And yet this is where I was ordered to go for 'treatment' to 'raise my self-esteem.' Some women had been away from their ex's for six to eight years, yet continued to go to the meetings. It was like their victimhood was an all encompassing identity. They were addicted to being a 'victim' so people would feel sorry for them." Moore goes on to argue that support groups cultivate this sense of perpetual victimhood to maintain clients so that the organizations can continue to get government funding.

Women's shelters and support groups are just some of the existing community-based responses to the problem of domestic violence. The authors in the following chapter examine the effectiveness of other social service programs designed to curb domestic violence.

"Screening for abuse enables patients to recognize a problem, even if they are not ready for help at that point."

Medical Professionals Should Screen Patients for Domestic Abuse

Mallika Punukollu

In the following article, Mallika Punukollu, a doctor in England, insists that medical professionals should routinely screen their patients for signs of domestic abuse. Punukollu maintains that identifying abuse can help patients recognize dangerous relationships and seek community services quickly. Although all medical professionals can assist abuse victims, personal physicians have a more trusting relationship with their patients and can therefore help any victims of abuse with developing safety plans, obtaining local services, or discussing the matter with the police. Punukollu notes that it is important for doctors to be familiar with various methods of screening and to be aware of the community services (such as shelters, support groups, etc.) in their areas for immediate referral.

As you read, consider the following questions:
1. According to Punukollu, how much greater are abuse victim's outpatient costs than nonvictim's costs?
2. According to Punukollu, two studies in the 1990s found that what type of screening procedure is better than patient interviews?

Mallika Punukollu, "Domestic Violence Screen Made Practical," *Journal of Family Practice*, July 2003. Copyright © 2003 by the *Journal of Family Practice*. Reproduced by permission.

D omestic violence is a chronic life-threatening condition that is treatable. If abuse is left untreated, the severity and frequency of abuse can worsen, leading to serious adverse effects to health and potentially life-threatening consequences. However, if we identify victims by screening and offer information including safety plans and referrals to advocacy services, the prognosis is improved in terms of reported quality of life and fewer violence-related injuries.

Although the effectiveness of screening on every aspect of the recovery process has not been validated by randomized controlled trials, the current literature certainly suggests likely benefit in certain stages. Qualitative evidence from abuse victims supports the assumption that screening for abuse enables patients to recognize a problem, even if they are not ready for help at that point.

Prevalence of Domestic Violence

A [1995] study by the Centers for Disease Control and Prevention of 1,691,600 women found that 30% had experienced domestic violence during their lifetimes. The prevalence of domestic violence is difficult to measure due to different definitions of abuse and factors that preclude accurate reporting by victims, such as safety and social stigma.

One [1992] anonymous survey in a family practice setting found that 23% of women had been physically assaulted by their partners in the past year, and another [1995] anonymous survey of 1,952 female patients attending 4 different community-based primary care practices found that 1 of every 5 had experienced violence in their adult lives.

Domestic violence is also a financial burden to victims and to society: domestic violence victims have 2.5 times greater outpatient costs than do nonvictims.

Why Screen All Women?

Particular history and physical findings are associated with increased likelihood of domestic violence (Table 1). Neither victims nor batterers fit a distinct personality or profile, however, and abuse affects women of all ages, ethnicities, and socioeconomic classes. Predicting which women will be affected is difficult, which suggests that universal screening is more appropriate than targeting specific groups. . . .

The American Academy of Family Physicians, the American College of Physicians, the American Medical Association, and the American College of Obstetricians and Gynecologists all recommend screening for domestic violence. Screening does increase the detection of domestic violence. The screening can be a questionnaire filled out by the patient or a directed interview conducted by a staff member or physician. Two recent studies [1991, 1999] found that questionnaires are better than interviews at detecting domestic violence.

Table 1: History and Physical Findings Suggestive of Abuse

- Inconsistent explanation of injuries or delay in seeking treatment
- Somatic [physical] complaints
- Psychiatric illness
- Frequent visits to the emergency room
- Injuries, especially to head and neck
- Low birth weight

The Joint Commission on Accreditation of Healthcare Organizations now mandates that all hospitals screen patients for domestic violence. Educating health care providers about domestic violence and screening improves their self-reported ability to identify and manage abuse victims. In addition, screening for domestic violence increases the rate of referrals to community resources. Administrative changes, guidelines, protocols, and changes to standardized medical record forms to assist screening for domestic violence increase identification of victims and help maintain sustained change in screening behavior over more than 12 months.

Useful Screening Instruments

New screening tools are briefer and more efficient than earlier devices.

The HITS Scale (Hurt, Insult, Threaten, Scream) (Table 2) is a practical 4-item scale. It has been validated in the family practice setting in a study that compared 160 family practice patients whose abuse status was unknown with 99 self-identified victims of abuse.

Table 2: The HITS Scale

Hurt	How often does your partner physically hurt you?
Insult	How often does your partner insult or talk down to you?
Threaten	How often does your partner threaten you with physical harm?
Scream	How often does your partner scream or curse at you?

Each question is answered on a 5-point scale: 1 = never, 2 = rarely, 3 = sometimes, 4 = fairly often, 5 = frequently. The score ranges from 4 to a maximum of 20. A score of [greater than or equal to] 10 is considered diagnostic of abuse.

The Woman Abuse Screening Tool (WAST) was developed for the family practice setting. It was validated by a study comparing the responses between 24 self-identified abused women from shelters and 24 nonabused women recruited from the principal investigator's professional contacts.

The first 2 questions of the WAST screen make up the WAST-short questions:

1. In general, how would you describe your relationship? (A lot of tension; some tension; no tension)
2. Do you and your partner work out arguments with . . . ? (great difficulty; some difficulty; no difficulty)

These questions assess the degree of relationship tension and the amount of difficulty the patient and her partner have in working out arguments. If a patient answers affirmatively to these 2 questions, then the physician can use the remaining WAST questions to elicit more information about the patient's experience of abuse. A Spanish version of the WAST has been shown to be successful as well.

The WAST and HITS scales need to be further evaluated prospectively in larger populations with a high prevalence of abuse. In addition, nonbiased samples need to be recruited and the tests need to be validated against a criterion standard.

The HITS scale has been tested in English-speaking populations only. The ability to screen different ethnic groups and ask sensitive questions across cultural barriers is important and should be studied further.

The Women's Experience with Battering Scale is a series of 10 questions tested in a large cross-sectional survey of women (n=1,152) attending 1 of 2 family practice clinics. It has been validated in a study using the Index of Spouse Abuse as a reference standard (18% of the women surveyed had experienced violence in a current or most recent intimate relationship with a male partner). For every 100 female patients seen, a physician will correctly identify 16 of 18 abuse victims and will incorrectly label 7 nonabused women as victims. For this reason, a positive screen using any instrument must be followed-up by a careful interview before further intervention.

Unlike other tests, the Women's Experience with Battering Scale was conducted in a relatively larger, unbiased, sample population, had good accuracy, and is recommended. The only drawback is the length, but it can be self-administered as part of a routine intake for an annual health maintenance examination. . . .

How Physicians Can Help Ensure Safety

The care of the abused woman requires a multidisciplinary team approach involving institutional and community services. The literature suggests that once a victim of abuse is identified in an office setting, a primary care physician can improve outcome by caring for acute injuries, offering support, and making appropriate referrals.

A physician can help ensure safety by:
- Assessing immediate risk. Has the violence increased in frequency or severity over the past year? Has your partner threatened to kill you or your children? Are there weapons in the house? Does your partner know that you are planning to leave?

  If immediate risk appears high, then it is important to emphasize to the patient that her situation could be life-threatening, to explain her options, and to encourage immediate referral to community resources with assistance from security and law enforcement, if necessary.

- Discussing safety behaviors. This includes advice on self-protection (i.e., removal of weapons from the home) and planning for leaving safely in a threatening situation. One study of abused pregnant mothers found that receiving a safety intervention protocol significantly increased the safety behaviors adopted during and after pregnancy, preventing further abuse and increasing the safety and well-being of mother and baby.
- Helping the patient obtain a civil protection order. This can be obtained with the assistance of the police or community advocacy services. Women with permanent protection orders are less likely than those without orders to be physically abused.
- A trusting relationship with the patient can help her break the cycle of abuse and enable her to change her circumstances. A qualitative study [in 2002] showed that battered women have rated the following behaviors highly desirable in their physicians.

> Initially validates their experiences with compassionate messages and emphasizes their worth as human beings.

> Clearly labels the abuse as wrong and criminal.

> Listens in a careful, nonjudgmental manner.

Having someone to confide in and having told someone about the abuse were factors associated with diminished abuse at 3 months in one study.

Referral to Community Resources

A randomized controlled trial with 2-year follow-up investigated community-based advocacy for abused women who were leaving a shelter program. This study found that advocacy services led to significantly greater effectiveness in obtaining resources, a decrease in physical violence, a decrease in depression, and an improved quality of life and social support at 10 weeks post-shelter. At 2 years, advocacy services led to reduced physical violence, increased likelihood of leaving the abusive relationship, and improved quality of life.

[H.E.] Straus and colleagues associated contact with community domestic violence resources with a decreased sense of community isolation. The National Domestic Violence Hotline (800-799-SAFE) can provide physicians in every state with information on local resources.

[R.L.] Muelleman and [K.M.] Feighny found that advocacy programs that are available on-site can improve the use of shelters and shelter-based counseling. However, there are no studies of suitable quality comparing outcomes for women using shelters with women not using shelters. Bias-free samples would be difficult to recruit. One study that evaluated experiences before and after shelter found that women experienced less violence after the shelter stay.

"In two surveys of health professionals only a minority of doctors and half of nurses were in favour of screening."

Screening Patients for Domestic Abuse Is Ineffective

Jean Ramsay, Jo Richardson, Yvonne H. Carter, Leslie L. Davidson, and Gene Feder

In the following viewpoint, Jean Ramsay and colleagues examine the results of patient screening by medical professionals. The authors contend that, despite the health-care profession's optimistic outlook on patient screening, very few studies have analyzed the outcomes of this type of intervention on the lives of patients experiencing domestic abuse. While screening programs have increased the identification of abuse cases, there is no evidence that the recognition of abuse and subsequent referral to outside services had any positive impact on patients' well-being. Jean Ramsay and colleagues are all associated with the Department of General Practice and Primary Care at Queen Mary's School of Medicine and Dentistry, University of London.

As you read, consider the following questions:
1. According to Ramsay and colleagues, what four assumptions are made in recommending that health-care professionals routinely screen patients?
2. What fraction of patients found screening acceptable, according to the authors' overall analysis?
3. In the authors' opinion, should health-care professionals abandon identifying domestic abuse in patients? Why?

Jean Ramsay, Jo Richardson, Yvonne H. Carter, Leslie L. Davidson, and Gene Feder, "Should Health Professionals Screen Women for Domestic Violence? Systemic Review," *British Medical Journal*, August 10, 2002. Copyright © 2002 by the *British Medical Journal*. Reproduced by permission.

Violence against women by male partners and ex-partners is a major public health problem, resulting in injuries and other short term and long term health consequences, including mental illness and complications of pregnancy. Exposure of children to domestic violence results in emotional, behavioural, and health problems. The response of health services to domestic violence is an international priority. In the United Kingdom many organisations of health professionals have published guidelines or recommendations. These guidelines are not identical, but they all emphasise the prevalence of domestic violence and advocate recognition, assessment, and referral within and beyond the health service. The Department of Health in England now recommends that health professionals should consider "routine enquiry" of some or all women patients for a history of domestic violence. This is essentially a recommendation to screen women for domestic violence in healthcare settings and echoes long-standing recommendations of organisations and accreditation bodies in North America.

Implicit in these recommendations to undertake screening is the assumption that this will increase identification of women who are experiencing violence, lead to appropriate interventions and support, and ultimately decrease exposure to violence and its detrimental health consequences, both physical and psychological. These assumptions underlie the justification for conventional screening for the premorbid or early stage of a disease. A further assumption of the recommendations is that health professionals and female patients alike will not object to the screening process. In this review we test these assumptions.

Searching Through Recent Studies

We used medical subject headings and text words to search for studies on three bibliographic databases: . . . We found 2520 potentially relevant English language studies with on-line abstracts.

We eventually retrieved 112 full papers. Twenty papers met the inclusion criteria; we excluded the remaining 92 papers.

We applied the results of the studies to three review questions: Do women patients and health professionals find screening for domestic violence acceptable? Do screening programmes increase the identification of women who are experiencing domestic violence? Do interventions with women identified in healthcare settings improve outcomes? We did not combine the results of the studies because of the heterogeneity of interventions, outcomes, and populations. In our narrative analysis we consider the results in relation to the design and quality of the studies.

We found few good quality studies that addressed our review questions. Generally, details of methods, interventions, and results were poorly described in the papers we reviewed. We did not find any randomised controlled trials of interventions based in healthcare settings to improve outcomes. The range of outcomes was limited, and no studies measured potential risk to women of identification from screening in healthcare settings and subsequent management by health professionals. Another potential limitation of the primary studies, from the perspective of European healthcare policy, is their geographical distribution: most were from North America, with three papers from Australia or New Zealand.

Study Results

Details of the five studies assessing attitudes to screening are available on [the *British Medical Journal* website] bmj.com. Four studies elicited the views of women patients about screening. In two of these studies three quarters or more of the respondents thought that routine screening was acceptable, with no significant difference between abused and non-abused respondents. In the other two studies just under half of all women found screening acceptable, with abused women in one of the studies being one and a half times more likely to favour this course of action. The heterogeneity of these results may be partly explained by the wording of the question about screening in the different surveys. In particular, the two studies reporting lower acceptability asked if screening at all consultations was acceptable, whereas the studies reporting a higher acceptability asked a more general question. As far as health professionals are concerned, one study of primary care physicians in New England found one third to be in favour of routine screening. In a study of emergency department nurses 53% responded that nurses should routinely screen all women for a history of domestic violence.

Our conclusions regarding identification of women experiencing domestic violence are drawn from nine studies (10 papers). Details of these studies are available on bmj.com. The studies were mostly based in the United States, with one each in Australia, New Zealand, and Canada. Most of the studies tested the effect of applying a screening protocol containing up to five questions about abuse to all women presenting in emergency departments, primary care facilities, or antenatal clinics. Baseline rates of identification were mostly in a range of 0–3%.

Screening produced an increase in rates of identification in eight of the studies, but not in the study with the strongest design. Screening typically resulted in doubling of identification rates, but larger effect sizes were detected in three of the studies. The most robust of the parallel group studies measured a sevenfold increase in the identification of abused women, although the small sample size resulted in wide confidence intervals for this estimate. Most of the studies did not monitor identification rates beyond an initial measurement after the screening protocol or programme had been implemented. One study that did measure identification rates in an emergency department one year after implementation of a protocol found that an initial improvement in comparison with a control department was not sustained. Screening programmes that provided substantial additional educational and training sessions for staff did not identify a higher proportion of women experiencing abuse. Programmes with multiple screening questions did not produce larger effects than those using single questions.

Intervention Success Rates

Six studies (nine papers) fulfilled our criteria—five from the United States and one from New Zealand. Details of these studies are available on bmj.com. None was a randomised controlled trial, the method least prone to bias for testing the effectiveness of a health service intervention. The interventions in antenatal clinics, primary care, and emergency departments included advice about services, advocacy, and counselling. We found no relation between type of intervention or type of healthcare setting and the effect of the intervention on measured outcomes.

Only two of the studies measured rates of domestic violence as outcomes. The more robust of these, which used a parallel group design and adjusted for differences in baseline rates and potential confounding factors, detected a reduction of physical and non-physical abuse with counselling and advocacy support for women identified in antenatal clinics. The other study that measured violence as an outcome was based in an emergency department. The investigators used a weaker (time series) design and measured visits to an emergency department for injury from domestic violence rather than reports from participants. The study did not detect a reduction in violence to participants after an advocacy based intervention.

Four studies measured referral to other agencies, and all but one found increased referral.

Obstacles to Screening

We found that about half to three quarters of women patients in primary care responding to surveys think that screening for domestic violence in healthcare settings is acceptable, with a higher proportion among women who have experienced abuse. In two surveys of health professionals only a minority of doctors and half of nurses were in favour of screening. A recent study in the United Kingdom, published after the time limit of this review, also found that a minority of health professionals wish to screen women for a history of domestic violence. A systematic review of studies of barriers to screening for domestic violence found that healthcare professionals gave a range of reasons for not routinely asking women about domestic violence: lack of education in or experience of screening, fear of offending or endangering patients, lack of effective interventions, patients not disclosing or not complying with screening, and limited time.

In our review we found that screening programmes generally increased rates of identification of women experiencing domestic violence in antenatal and primary care clinics and emergency departments. This concurs with [J.] Waalen et al's [2000] review of studies evaluating interventions designed to increase screening for domestic violence. That review also included interventions that consisted solely of education of professionals, without specific screening protocols or questions; educating professionals about domestic violence did not result in increased identification of women experiencing abuse. On the whole, the magnitude of improved identification as a result of a screening programme was modest, and we found no evidence that the improvements were sustained, as most of the studies did not measure rates beyond initial implementation.

We found little evidence for the effectiveness of interventions in healthcare settings with women who are identified by screening programmes. Randomised controlled trials are lacking, as are studies that measure important outcomes for participants, such as quality of life or mental health status. Rates of referral to outside agencies are not a convincing proxy. The primary studies we reviewed did not measure possible harm that may result from interventions initiated in healthcare settings.

Weakness of Current Studies

The screening studies and intervention studies that we reviewed had substantial methodological weaknesses. All but one relied on parallel group or longitudinal [over time] designs. Most were underpowered, with only five out of nine identification studies and one out of six intervention studies justifying their sample size. No study considered possible bias in measuring outcomes. Generally, papers gave insufficient detail about data collection and analysis and about the content of the screening programme or intervention. Despite these weaknesses in the primary studies, we can still conclude that a screening protocol or programme will probably increase identification, at least in the short term, and that little evidence exists for the effectiveness of interventions.

Identification Does Not Lead to Effective Intervention

From the studies we reviewed, even without considering all the criteria for a screening programme, we conclude that it would be premature to introduce a screening programme for domestic violence in healthcare settings. We know that introducing a programme is likely to increase the number of women experiencing domestic violence who are identified by health professionals, but not that subsequent interventions are effective. In order to base healthcare policy for domestic violence on evidence of safety and effectiveness we need to answer several research questions (Table 1). In particular, research funders should give priority to randomised controlled trials of interventions in healthcare settings to test their effectiveness and safety for women and their families.

Table 1: Research Questions

- What are the benefits and risks to women of screening for domestic violence in healthcare settings?

- What is the most effective screening interval?

- What is the effect of participation in interventions such as provision of advocacy support on women experiencing domestic violence identified in healthcare settings?

- What are the training needs of health professionals in relation to domestic violence?

- How can we promote better multi-agency working in this area?

Our conclusions about the effectiveness of screening should not be interpreted as a denial of domestic violence as an important issue for healthcare providers. Debate is taking place among physicians in the United States regarding the validity of policies on domestic violence, partly because of lack of evidence for the effectiveness of screening. However, a strong consensus exists among healthcare organisations internationally that doctors and nurses should not abandon the goal of identifying and supporting women experiencing domestic violence. The high prevalence and severity of the problem and the views of women themselves require a response from health services. Health professionals need education and training to remain aware of the problem if they are to recognise women who experience domestic violence. Health services, local authorities, and the police need to coordinate their responses to domestic violence, but research is essential to develop and evaluate interagency policies. Finally, women's organisations have been instrumental in raising public and institutional awareness of domestic violence. These organisations should be involved in future policy decisions and the development of health service–based interventions.

*"A variety of reasons can be offered for
providing couples therapy for domestic
violence."*

Couples Counseling Can Reduce Domestic Violence

Sandra M. Stith, Karen H. Rosen, and Eric E. McCollum

Sandra M. Stith, Karen H. Rosen, and Eric E. McCollum argue that couples counseling for domestic violence cases can be effective if counselors are experienced and have ascertained that the therapy is not likely to bring further abuse upon the victim. In the following viewpoint, Stith, Rosen, and Mc-Collum admit that couples counseling is not appropriate in all domestic violence cases, but they insist that in some instances, such as when there is mutual violence in a relationship, addressing the issue as a couple may be helpful. Professor Sandra M. Stith is the program director for the Marriage and Family Therapy department at Virginia Polytechnic Institute and State University, Falls Church, Virginia. Karen H. Rosen and Eric E. McCollum also work in that department. Rosen is an assistant professor. McCollum is an associate professor and clinical director of the department.

As you read, consider the following questions:

1. What are "parallel track" treatment programs, and why are they the most common forms of treatment?
2. Identify three of the reasons that couples counseling may be more effective in treating domestic violence than other treatment methods.
3. What did F.W. Dunford's 2000 experimental study of conjoint treatment reveal?

Sandra M. Stith, Karen H. Rosen, and Eric E. McCollum, "Effectiveness of Couples Treatment for Spouse Abuse," *Journal of Marital and Family Therapy*, July 2003. Copyright © 2003 by the American Association for Marriage & Family Therapy. Reproduced by permission.

D espite its controversy, carefully conceptualized and delivered couples treatment appears to be at least as effective as traditional treatment for domestic violence, and preliminary data suggests that it does not place women at greater risk for injury. However, the body of research on which these conclusions rest is sparse. Only six experimental studies have been done, each using different eligibility criteria, outcome measures, and treatment approaches. Thus, further study of this modality is warranted. Marriage and family therapists have an important part to play in continuing to develop and test innovative ways of helping couples end violence and improve their relationships—an endeavor that promises to improve the quality of the partners' lives as well as those of their children. . . .

A Controversial Treatment

Although historically spouse abuse has been viewed as a private family matter, it is now viewed as a societal problem as well as a crime subject to legal punishment. This paradigmatic shift in perspective has brought a great deal of change in how spouse abuse is handled in our communities. Whereas legal authorities were once reluctant to intervene in violence that was thought to be a private matter between partners, perpetrators now are often faced with jail time or mandatory treatment. Two clear messages emerge: the aggressor must be held accountable, and the victim must be protected. Beyond these two primary concerns, spouse abuse treatment goals vary according to the theoretical perspective of the treatment program. Currently most programs for offenders and all treatment programs that have been formally evaluated are designed for male offenders. Most treatment is administered to men in groups, while concurrent support services and treatment for women victims and their children are offered. This model of "parallel track" treatment is based on the belief that conjoint treatment will increase the danger to victims of abuse by forcing them to confront their abusers directly, will increase the emotional intensity of the couple relationship which may also lead to violence, and will suggest that the victim is at least partially responsible for her abuse because she is being asked to make changes in relationship patterns along with the perpetrator. Although a number of investigators have begun to explore ways to work with couples safely and productively, couples treatment remains controversial. . . .

Reciprocal Violence, Conjoint Treatment

Although controversy exists about the appropriateness of treating violent couples together, a variety of reasons can be offered for providing couples therapy for domestic violence. First, a consistent research finding is that male batterers are a heterogeneous group. . . .

From the growing domestic violence typology literature, it has become increasingly clear that all batterers do not need the same type of treatment. Most clinicians and researchers that advocate the use of conjoint approaches suggest that it should be limited to one subtype of batterer—the family-only batterer without apparent psychopathy, who is most likely to benefit from couples therapy.

In addition to treating subgroups of batterers differently, there is also reason to include female partners in treatment. Both men and women are often violent in relationships. In fact, most research has found that women initiate and carry out physical assaults on their partners as often as do men. Despite the much lower probability of physical injury resulting from attacks by women, assaults by women are serious, just as it would be serious if men "only" slapped their wives or "only" slapped female fellow employees. If reciprocal violence is taking place in relationships, treating men without treating women is not likely to stop the violence. In fact, cessation of partner violence by one partner is highly dependent on whether the other partner also stops hitting. Most importantly, when women use violence in relationships, they are at greater risk of being severely assaulted by their partners. Moreover, although men's treatment groups address men's role in intimate partner violence, they do not address any underlying relationship dynamics that may impact each partner's decision to remain in the violent relationship despite the violence, or may play a part in maintaining the violence. Because 50% to 70% of battered wives remain with their abusive partners or return to them after leaving a women's shelter or otherwise separating from them, failing to provide services to both parties in an ongoing relationship may inadvertently disadvantage the female partner who chooses to stay. . . .

[F.W.] Dunford (2000) conducted the only experimental study that included a conjoint treatment condition and a "no treatment" control group. He randomly assigned 861 Navy couples to one of four interventions: a 26-week cognitive behavioral therapy (CBT) men's group followed by six monthly sessions, a 26-week CBT multi-couple group followed by six monthly sessions, a "rigorously monitored" group, and a control group. The control group did not receive any formal intervention. Victimized wives in the control group were contacted by the military agency responsible for preventing and responding to domestic violence—the Family Advocacy Center (FAC)—as soon as possible after the presenting incident to ensure that the women were not in immediate danger of continued abuse. Once their safety was assured, FAC provided wives with safety planning information. No other formal intervention was offered.

In the rigorously monitored group, a case manager at the FAC saw perpetrators monthly for 12 months and provided individual counseling. Every 6 weeks a record search was completed to determine if perpetrators had been arrested or referred to court anywhere in San Diego County. Wives were called monthly and asked about repeat abuse. They were told that they did not have to reveal anything about their husband's behavior if doing so would place them in jeopardy. At the end of each treatment session, case managers sent progress reports to perpetrators and their commanding officers, specifying the presence or absence of instances of abuse. This process of rigorous monitoring was an attempt to create a "fishbowl" for perpetrators in which they felt that any instance of repeat abuse would be identified and dealt with by the military authorities. . . .

FAC records indicated that 71% of the cases were judged as having successfully completed treatment. Fifteen percent of the men were discharged from the Navy and therefore did not complete treatment. The remainder of the cases (14%) were considered as not having completed treatment. Thus, a conservative estimate of the dropout rate would be 29% if those leaving the Navy were defined as dropouts along with those labeled "not completing treatment." Analysis of the data revealed that 83% of the men completing treatment (men's, conjoint, and rigorous monitoring) did not re-injure their wives during a 1-year follow-up period. Because 79% of the men in the control group also did not re-injure their wives, there were no significant differences between groups on rate of re-injury. Findings also revealed no significant differences between groups on a variety of other outcome measures including "being pushed or hit," sexual abuse, and control abuse. Thus, in the military setting, the no-treatment group seemed to do as well as the treatment groups. . . .

Who May Benefit from Counseling

Some battered women prefer couples counseling. Current thinking in much of the domestic violence field is that battered women know what is best for them. After all, battered women have a track record of survival, and they—more than professionals—are able to judge their own safety. . . .

Promoters of couple groups for men who batter and their partners now attend more to victim safety, largely because of criticism by advocates that couples counseling puts battered women at risk. Often, men in couples counseling are staked in conformity, less violent, and not violent outside the family; consequently, they are more motivated to complete the program.

Larry W. Bennett and Oliver J. Williams, "Men Who Batter," in Robert L. Hampton, ed., *Family Violence: Prevention and Treatment.* 2nd ed. Vol. 1. Thousand Oaks, CA: Sage, 1999.

Although Dunford's (2000) findings have limited usefulness in evaluating couples treatment, they did demonstrate that adding wives to a males' treatment group did not increase the risk to the wives. Wives participating in the conjoint groups were no more likely to be assaulted or injured than wives whose husbands participated only in men's treatment.

One early study ([R.] Harris et al., 1988) randomly assigned 81 couples that had contacted a family-service agency requesting relationship counseling to a multi-couple group treatment program or to couples counseling. Although the authors indicate that they also had a waiting-list control group, they do not compare the outcome of the treatment groups to the outcome of the control group. To be eligible for the program, a man had to use physical and/or sexual violence toward his partner or property and frighten or control her. The woman (when interviewed individually) had to indicate that she wished to remain in the relationship and report that she did not feel endangered. Furthermore, the man had to exhibit no psychotic symptoms, no evidence of serious brain injury, and no pervasive substance abuse that was not being treated concurrently.

The multi-couple group program consisted of 10 weekly 3-hour sessions. During the first 90 minutes of each session, the men and women met separately in same-sex peer groups. The women's group focused on the process of ending victimization, and the men's group concentrated on confronting violent behaviors and understanding attitudes that contribute to controlling behavior. Afterwards, the men and women met together with both group leaders for 1-hour teaching sessions on topics that included time-out procedures and the cycle of violence. Two review sessions were held at 1 month and 4 months after the program ended.

The individual couples counseling program was a "family systems–based form of treatment modified so that the therapist explicitly addressed the violence against the woman as the primary problem in the relationship using concepts developed in the group program." Treatment in this condition continued until the couple and therapist mutually agreed that all goals had been accomplished.

Sixty-seven percent of the 35 couples assigned to individual couples counseling dropped out before completing treatment, whereas only 16% of the 23 couples assigned to the multi-couple group dropped out. Only a small number of the initial couples completed all pre and post measures (5 couples who had completed couples counseling; 16 couples who participated in the multi-couple group). Repeated-measures analysis of variance indicated that scores on all aspects of psychological well-being assessed (i.e., levels of violence, mood states, self-confidence, and social support) did not vary by treatment group or by sex, but that participants' mean pre-

and post-tests scores for all the measures were significantly different; that is, participants showed positive changes over time, regardless of sex or treatment group. Follow-up results revealed that the goal of stopping the physical violence was achieved for over 80% of the couples based on reports by women who participated in the follow-up interview, and that these results did not differ by treatment group. . . .

Violence between partners in intimate relationships is a complex and troubling phenomenon, one that challenges our conceptions of love and intimate relationships and exacts an immense toll in human suffering and social costs. In order to bring domestic violence out from behind the wall of "private family matters," advocates for battered women some 30 years ago took a strong and uncompromising stance that all violence against women is best dealt with as a crime, that it reflects the patriarchal nature of society, and that any attempt to examine couple dynamics in domestic violence adds to battered women's victimization. At the same time, some aspects of domestic violence were, of necessity, left out of the advocacy movement's analysis.

In order to advance an important social change agenda, advocates downplayed the prevalence of female assaults on male partners; the wish many victims have to stay with abusive partners, albeit without continued violence; the different subgroups of batterers, each of which might need a different intervention approach; and the possibility that conjoint treatment could help end violence and empower women in their relationship without suggesting they are responsible for being abused. Over the past 10 years, researchers and treatment professionals have begun to consider these issues in more depth, with a growing interest in conjoint couples therapy being one result.

*"While [counseling] courses were well-
intentioned . . . , they ignore the dynamics
of domestic violence, which is about power
and control over another."*

Couples Counseling Does Not Reduce Domestic Violence

Khurram Saeed

Perpetrators of domestic violence are often required to participate in couples counseling. In the following selection, Khurram Saeed, a writer for the *Journal News* in Westchester, New York, describes an effort to end this practice in Rockland County, New York. According to Saeed, the current prevailing attitude in Rockland is that domestic violence is not something that can be worked out in counseling. Saeed reports that most advocates of the policy change fear that counseling may lead to further abuse or may make the victims feel as if they share in the blame for domestic violence.

As you read, consider the following questions:

1. Why does Justice William Warren believe anger management and counseling courses are ineffective?
2. According to Saeed, what did most Rockland advocates of the new policy believe was the most effective way to stop domestic abuse?
3. As cited by Saeed, what erroneous messages do counseling sessions often convey to victims of abuse?

Rockland's judges in domestic violence cases should stop requiring couples counseling or anger management programs because they do not help and may put the abused partner in danger, an advocacy group said yesterday.

The proposed policy was announced at a meeting of the STOP FEAR Coalition, which involves police, prosecutors, judges, mental health professionals, social service workers and advocates for battered women. Established in 1986, the coalition coordinates the county's overall efforts against domestic violence, whose victims are mostly women.

The policy is expected to be put into practice by the 37 judges who serve in county, town, village and family courts, although judges will decide for themselves whether or when to implement it.

The Need for Zero Tolerance

There are nearly 350 cases involving domestic violence in Rockland each year, county District Attorney Michael Bongiorno said.

Nationwide, a woman is beaten by a man every 18 seconds, the FBI said. The bureau's statistics also show a woman is killed every 22 days in a domestic violence incident.

The public policy was created by STOP FEAR's judicial subcommittee as another way to protect victims from more violence and to require the justice system to punish the abuser appropriately.

Anger management programs and couples counseling are sometimes requested, generally by the defense attorney, in court.

Rockland Family Court Justice William Warren, who chairs the judicial subcommittee, said while the courses were well-intentioned, and useful in other criminal cases, they ignore the dynamics of domestic violence, which is about power and control over another.

"Perpetrators of domestic violence do not have, in my opinion, an anger management problem," Warren said at the meeting, held at United Hospice of Rockland's New City headquarters. "They do not blow up and explode because something triggers them. They act very deliberately. They act in a very controlled way."

Advocates said zero tolerance was the most effective way to stop domestic violence. Those methods include jail time, probation and court orders of protection.

An Unrealistic Strategy

STOP FEAR co-founder Carolyn Fish, executive director of the Rockland Family Shelter, the county's only shelter for battered women, said the county has always been at the fore-front of creating and implementing changes to address domestic violence.

In 1985, Fish and STOP FEAR co-founder Phyllis Frank worked with local police departments to require officers to arrest those suspected of abusing their partner without the victim's filing a complaint. State law didn't make such arrests mandatory until 1994.

Schwadron. © 1996 by Harley Schwadron. Reproduced by permission.

Warren said couples counseling was once thought to be an effective way for partners to "work things out" and "talk it over."

But meaningful dialogue between partners can't take place when abuse is occurring, he said. People who are hit or intimidated and being encouraged to speak openly about their partner's behavior in their presence are inadvertently put in harm's way.

"They can suffer retaliation," said Warren, adding that judges should make it a point to explain these reasons in court when a victim suggests counseling.

Advocates also said victims often take responsibility during the sessions for bringing on the violence, thus shifting accountability from the batterer to the victim.

Expanding the New Policy

Clarkstown Justice Joel Flick, who oversees the town's year-old domestic violence court, said when a defendant asks to enter such a program, it gives the abused partner the message that "I'm going to change," which often proves not to be the case. The Clarkstown domestic violence court, the only one of its kind in the state, has handled 117 since June.

Of the 350 domestic violence cases the District Attorney's Office prosecutes annually, more than 300 are handled in town and village courts as misdemeanor charges, including assaults, harassments and violations of court orders of protection. Felony cases are handled in County Court.

Joseph Suarez, president of the Rockland County Magistrates Association, said most judges in the county have moved away from ordering couples counseling. However, he said judges still tend to favor anger management classes.

Suarez, who is also Chestnut Ridge village justice, said the new policy would be given to the organization's members. While it is not binding, he said it will be strongly recommended that they follow it.

Charlotte Watson, executive director of the New York State Office for the Prevention of Domestic Violence, who also attended the meeting, said she would work to have the Rockland policy used throughout the state.

Periodical Bibliography

The following articles have been selected to supplement the diverse views presented in this chapter.

Janice Asher et al.
"Detection and Treatment of Domestic Violence," *Contemporary OB/GYN*, September 2001.

C.C. Bell and J. Mathis
"The Importance of Cultural Competence in Ministering to African American Victims of Domestic Violence," *Violence Against Women*, May 2000.

Deborah I. Bybee and Cris M. Sullivan
"The Process Through Which an Advocacy Intervention Resulted in Positive Change for Battered Women over Time," *American Journal of Community Psychology*, February 2002.

Kathryn Andersen Clark et al.
"Who Gets Screened During Pregnancy for Partner Violence?" *Archives of Family Medicine*, November 2000.

Thomas B. Cole
"Is Domestic Violence Screening Helpful?" *JAMA*, August 2, 2000.

Victoria Stagg Elliott
"Doctors Make a Difference in Treating Abuse," *American Medical News*, July 22, 2002.

Janice Humphreys et al.
"Trauma History of Sheltered Battered Women," *Issues in Mental Health Nursing*, vol. 20, June 1, 1999.

M. Kerker
"Identification of Violence in the Home," *Journal of Developmental & Behavioral Pediatrics*, October 2000.

Demie Kurz
"Women, Welfare, and Domestic Violence," *Social Justice*, Spring 1998.

Garry Lapidus et al.
"A Statewide Survey of Domestic Violence Screening Behaviors Among Pediatricians and Family Physicians," *Archives of Pediatrics & Adolescent Medicine*, April 2002.

Candace Love et al.
"Dentists' Attitudes and Behaviors Regarding Domestic Violence: The Need for an Effective Response," *Journal of the American Dental Association*, January 2001.

Stephanie Riger and Maryann Krieglstein
"The Impact of Welfare Reform on Men's Violence Against Women," *American Journal of Community Psychology*, October 2000.

For Further Discussion

Chapter 1

1. Denise Kindschi Gosselin, Charles E. Corry, Amy Farmer, and Jill Tiefenthaler use a vast array of statistical studies to make their arguments about the seriousness and prevalence of domestic violence. Examine the various studies quoted in their viewpoints and determine how widespread you believe the problem of domestic violence is. Whose statistics do you think hold the most weight? Why? Is it possible that all the statistics are valid? If so, how can competing arguments exist?

2. The extent of female violence against men is hotly contested. Using Tara Rempel's and Christine Wicker's viewpoints, discuss how serious you think the problem is. Is it possible, as Rempel argues, that women "commit severe acts of violence against their partners almost twice as often as men do?" If you think this is accurate—or even if you believe men suffer an equal amount of domestic abuse—then why is the image of the battered male not more prevalent in media or popular culture?

Chapter 2

1. Amy J. Marin and Nancy Felipe Russo argue that male patriarchy is so entrenched in society that law enforcement and the courts—historically male domains—do not take domestic abuse seriously. Do you agree with Marin and Russo's conclusions? What, in your opinion, are the strengths of their assertions? What may be the weaknesses? Use arguments from any other viewpoint in the anthology to support your answers.

2. After reviewing the two articles debating the influence of alcohol on domestic violence, explain what role you think drinking might or might not play in the occurrence or severity of abuse. What dangers do Theresa M. Zubretsky and Karla M. Digirolamo see in making the link between alcohol and domestic violence? Is their argument persuasive? Explain.

3. After reading all the viewpoints in this chapter (and perhaps in the entire anthology), decide what factors (social, psychological, biological) you think might contribute to domestic violence and explain the connections as you see them. What factors mentioned in the chapter do not, in your opinion, influence domestic violence? Explain why these seem insignificant to you.

Chapter 3

1. In the two viewpoints on batterer prevention programs, both sets of authors note that these types of programs have had minimal success in changing batterers' views of abuse. Why do Larry W. Bennett and Oliver Williams see the minimal success as an indication that these programs should continue? Why do the researchers at the National Institute of Justice believe that the minimal success should prompt intervention strategists to revamp their programs? Using the evidence from the intervention program reports and the authors' arguments, explain which intervention models you would support (if any) and which (if any) you would change.

2. Examine the two viewpoints on mandatory reporting of domestic abuse. Imagine that you were an abuse patient at a doctor's office and argue why you would or would not want your doctor to report your injuries to the police. Would your arguments change if the setting was an emergency room and not your family doctor's office? Why or why not? Now imagine the same scenario but assume the role of the physician. Would your opinion on mandatory reporting change? Explain.

Chapter 4

1. Mallika Punukollu and Jean Ramsay and colleagues discuss routine medical screening of patients for signs of domestic abuse. Using the evidence these authors provide, discuss how you feel about screening. Does your opinion of screening change if you imagine yourself as the patient or the physician? Looking back at the articles on mandatory reporting in chapter three, explain what role (if any) you believe physicians should play in the fight against domestic abuse. In your answer, define what steps they should take and what limitations they should respect.

2. After reviewing the articles on couples counseling and medical screening, explain what social services may be effective in helping curb domestic violence. In drafting your answer, consider other social services not mentioned (such as the abuse shelter system) and research their effect on the issue. Do you think that social services might have a more significant impact on domestic violence than, for example, legal remedies? How do you think the two can work together to reduce domestic violence?

Organizations to Contact

The editors have compiled the following list of organizations concerned with the issues debated in this book. The descriptions are derived from materials provided by the organizations. All have publications or information available to interested readers. The list was compiled on the date of publication of the present volume; the information provided here may change. Be aware that many organizations take several weeks or longer to respond to inquiries, so allow as much time as possible.

Coalition for the Preservation of Fatherhood/Fatherhood Coalition (CPF)
PO Box 700, Milford, MA 01757
(617) 723-3237
e-mail: fathers-l@home.ease.lsoft.com
Web site: www.fatherhoodcoalition.org

Begun in 1993, the CPF is dedicated to fighting laws and public policy in which fatherhood or family unity is threatened. In terms of domestic violence, the CPF has taken the position that men are often unfairly blamed for the problem and that both men and women share the burden of finding a solution. The organization's Web site offers downloadable documents, several of which discuss domestic violence. There is also a reading room with other articles on the topic.

Emerge: Counseling and Education to Stop Domestic Violence
2464 Massachusetts Ave., Suite 101, Cambridge, MA 02140
(617) 547-9879 • fax: (617) 547-0904
e-mail: emergedv@aol.com • Web site: www.emergedv.com

Founded in 1977, Emerge works to increase public awareness of the causes of and solutions to domestic violence. Asserting that domestic abuse is a learned behavior, the organization also sponsors educational and counseling groups for fathers who want to be responsible partners and parents. The Web site has easily accessible information for batterers and victims as well as links to various services offered by Emerge. It also provides a means to purchase downloadable pamphlets and articles on domestic violence. A free newsletter is available on the Web site.

Family Research Laboratory (FRL)
University of New Hampshire
126 Horton Social Science Center, Durham, NH 03824
(603) 862-1888 • fax: (603) 862-1122
e-mail: mas2@christa.unh.edu • Web site: www.unh.edu/frl
The FRL does research on understanding family violence and its impact. The organization makes its findings available to the general public as well as policy makers. Since its inception in 1975, the FRL has published several books and hundreds of articles. Some of these are available from the organization at a cost.

Family Violence Prevention Fund (FVPF)
383 Rhode Island St., Suite 304, San Francisco, CA 94103
(415) 252-8900 • fax: (415) 252-8991
e-mail: info@endabuse.org • Web site: http://endabuse.org
FVPF is a nonprofit organization concerned with domestic violence education, prevention, and policy reform. It works to improve health care for battered women and to strengthen the judicial system's capacity to respond appropriately to domestic violence cases. The FVPF publishes brochures, action kits, and general information packets on domestic violence.

Independent Women's Forum (IWF)
1726 M St. NW, Suite 1001, Washington, DC 20036
(202) 419-1820
e-mail: info@iwf.org • Web site: www.iwf.org
The IWF is a conservative women's forum that advocates political freedom and personal responsibility for women. The organization has traditionally taken a stand against feminist interpretations of domestic violence, arguing that the issue is a social problem and not a male problem. A search of its Web site will reveal a host of opinion articles on domestic violence laws, research, and policy—many taken from its hard-copy publication, *Women's Quarterly.*

Men's Health Network (MHN)
PO Box 75972, Washington, DC 20013
(202) 543-6461 • fax: (202) 543-2727
e-mail: info@menshealthnetwork.org
Web site: www.menshealthnetwork.org
Founded in 1992, MHN is a nonprofit organization made up of physicians and other social science workers. The objective of MHN is to promote the health and well-being of men and boys. The MHN Web site includes a library with several documents pertaining to domestic violence, particularly as it relates to a perceived discrimination against men.

MenWeb

e-mail: berthoff@comcast.net • Web site: www.menweb.org

MenWeb is an Internet organization addressing men's issues. An entire Web page (www.batteredmen.com) is devoted to the issue of domestic abuse against men. There, visitors can find several articles on definitions of abuse, getting help for abuse victims, and an online pamphlet about domestic violence against men. MenWeb also publishes a hard-copy journal called *Men's Voices*.

Movement for the Establishment of Real Gender Equality (MERGE)

10011 116th St., Suite 501, Edmonton, AB T5K 1V4, Canada

(403) 488-4593

e-mail: Ferrel.Christensen@ualberta.ca

Web site: www.taiga.ca/~balance/mergprin.html

MERGE contends that publicity about family violence is biased toward women and ignores the male victims of spousal abuse. MERGE disseminates educational information on gender issues, including the pamphlet *Balancing the Approach to Spouse Abuse*. It also publishes a quarterly magazine entitled *Balance*.

National Clearinghouse for the Defense of Battered Women

125 South Ninth St., Suite 302, Philadelphia, PA 19107

(215) 351-0100 • fax: (215) 351-0779

Created in 1987, the clearinghouse provides assistance, resources, and support to battered women accused of killing or assaulting their abusers. Its publications include a newsletter entitled *Double-Time*.

National Coalition Against Domestic Violence (NCADV)

PO Box 18749, Denver, CO 80218

(303) 839-1852 • fax: (303) 831-9251

e-mail: mainoffice@ncadv.org • Web site: www.ncadv.org

Begun in 1978, the NCADV is a nationwide advocacy organization devoted to empowering battered women and their children. The group believes that violence against women results from an abuse of power in the home and in society; it therefore works with local, state, and national governments to create policies that will eliminate social conditions that contribute to violence. The NCADV has many pamphlets and fact sheets available from its Web site. Other publications, such as *Every Home a Safe Home* and *Teen Dating Violence Resource Manual*, are available through phone or mail order.

National Resource Center on Domestic Violence (NRCDV)
(800) 537-2238
Web site: www.nrcdv.org

Founded in 1993, the NRCDV offers technical assistance, training, and general information on domestic violence prevention. The organization works with state and local organizations to raise awareness and to end violence. It offers several papers and brochures that can be downloaded from the Web site and its links.

U.S. Department of Justice/Office on Violence Against Women
810 Seventh St. NW, Washington, DC 20531
(202) 307-6026 • fax: (202) 307-3911
Web site: www.ojp.usdoj.gov/vawo

The Office on Violence Against Women funds research reports on issues of violence against women and organizes advisory committees to shape governmental policy based on the mandates of the Violence Against Women Act. Its Web site contains easily accessed federal documents on domestic violence. The office also offers other publications such as *The Toolkit to End Violence Against Women.*

Bibliography of Books

Lundy Bancroft and Jay G. Silverman — *The Batterer as Parent: Addressing the Impact of Domestic Violence on Family Dynamics.* Thousand Oaks, CA: Sage, 2002.

Eve S. Buzawa and Carl G. Buzawa — *Domestic Violence: The Criminal Justice Response.* Thousand Oaks, CA: Sage, 2003.

Dorothy Ayers Counts, Judith K. Brown, and Jacquelyn C. Campbell — *To Have and to Hit: Cultural Perspectives on Wife Beating.* Urbana: University of Illinois Press, 1999.

Richard L. Davis — *Domestic Violence: Facts and Fallacies.* Westport, CT: Praeger, 1998.

Lynette Feder — *Women and Domestic Violence: An Interdisciplinary Approach.* New York: Haworth, 1999.

Marc Galanter, ed. — *Alcohol and Violence: Epidemiology, Neurobiology, Psychology, Family Issues.* New York: Kluwer Academic, 2002.

Lori B. Girshick — *Woman-to-Woman Violence: Does She Call It Rape?* Boston: Northeastern University Press, 2002.

Edward W. Gondolf — *Batterer Intervention Systems: Issues, Outcomes, and Recommendations.* Thousand Oaks, CA: Sage, 2002.

Denise Kindschi Gosselin — *Heavy Hands: An Introduction to the Crimes of Domestic Violence.* Upper Saddle River, NJ: Prentice-Hall, 2000.

Robert L. Hampton, ed. — *Family Violence: Prevention and Treatment.* 2nd ed. Vol. 1. Thousand Oaks, CA: Sage, 1999.

Michèle Harway and James M. O'Neil, eds. — *What Causes Men's Violence Against Women?* Thousand Oaks, CA: Sage, 1999.

Kerry M. Healey and Christine Smith — *Batterer Programs: What Criminal Justice Agencies Need to Know.* Washington, DC: U.S. Department of Justice, 1998.

Helen Henderson, ed. — *Domestic Violence and Child Abuse Sourcebook.* Detroit: Omnigraphics, 2000.

Carolyn Hoyle — *Negotiating Domestic Violence: Police, Criminal Justice, and Victims.* New York: Oxford University Press, 1998.

Neil S. Jacobson and John M. Gottman — *When Men Batter Women: New Insights into Ending Abusive Relationships.* New York: Simon & Schuster, 1998.

Sandra E. Lund and Beth Leventhal — *Same-Sex Domestic Violence.* Thousand Oaks, CA: Sage, 1999.

Ruth M. Mann   *Who Owns Domestic Abuse? The Local Politics of a
                        Social Problem.* Toronto, Canada: University of
                        Toronto Press, 2000.

Suellen Murray   *More than Refuge: Changing Responses to Domestic
                        Abuse.* Crawley: University of Western Australia
                        Press, 2002.

Albert R. Roberts, ed. *Handbook of Domestic Violence Intervention Strate-
                        gies: Policies, Programs, and Legal Remedies.* New
                        York: Oxford University Press, 2002.

Randal W. Summers   *Domestic Violence: A Global View.* Westport, CT:
and Allan M.   Greenwood, 2002.
Hoffman, eds.

Julie Taylor-Browne,   *What Works in Reducing Domestic Violence? A
ed.   Comprehensive Guide for Professionals.* Concord,
                        MA: Whiting & Birch, 2001.

Patricia Tjaden and   *Prevalence, Incidence, and Consequences of Violence
Nancy Thoennes   Against Women: Findings from the National Vio-
                        lence Against Women Survey.* Washington, DC:
                        U.S. Department of Justice, 1998.

Neil Websdale   *Rural Woman Battering and the Justice System: An
                        Ethnography.* Thousand Oaks, CA: Sage, 1998.

Joan Zorza, ed.   *Violence Against Women: Law, Prevention, Protec-
                        tion, Enforcement, Treatment, Health.* Kingston,
                        NJ: Civic Research Institute, 2002.

Index

Navy experiment (Dunford), 122–23
Neisen, J., 52

O'Malley, Nancy, 131
Ontario experiment (Palmer et al.),
    122–23
    study design and outcome of, 122

Pagelow, M.D., 57
Palmer, S.E., 121
patriarchy
    causes domestic violence, 68–75
    con, 76–81
    values of, 70
Pearson, Patricia, 34, 78
Pernanen, K., 84
Peterman, Linda M., 47
physicians
    attitudes of, on mandatory
        reporting, 140, 142
    intervention strategies of, 151–52
Pizzey, Erin, 29, 34, 80
polls. See surveys
poverty
    as major risk factor for domestic
        violence, 105, 108–10
    see also income
power dynamics, 72–73, 79
prevention programs, can curb
    domestic violence, 119–24
    con, 125–30
Prone to Violence (Pizzey), 34, 80
Punukollu, Mallika, 147

Quigley, Brian M., 82

racial differences
    in domestic violence against
        women, 18–19, 56, 58–59, 60–61
    in domestic violence arrest rates,
        74
Ramsay, Jean, 154
rape
    acquaintance/date, as precursor to
        spouse abuse, 24
    marital, correlation with other
        violence, 22
Rempel, Tara, 35
Rennison, C.M., 56
Renzetti, C.M., 49, 50
Richardson, Jo, 154
Roberts, Albert R., 23
Robinson, R.D., 42
Rodriguez, Michael A., 137
Rosen, Karen H., 162

Rosenbaum, Alan, 79
Rothery, Michael, 145
Russo, Nancy Felipe, 68, 72

Saeed, Khurram, 169
Scannell, Nancy, 14, 46
screening, for domestic abuse
    is ineffective, 154–61
    con, 147–53
    obstacles to, 158
    reasons for, 148–49
    research questions for, 160
    tools for, 149–51
Sewell, Bunny, 34, 78
Sewell, Sam, 34, 78
Sheaffer, Robert, 33
Sherman, Lawrence, 21
Smith, Jeffrey, 15
social isolation, as factor in domestic
    violence, 108–109
social learning theory, 66
Steinem, Gloria, 77
Steinmetz, Suzanne K., 23, 80
Stevens, Pat, 31
Stith, Sandra M., 162
Stockman, Farah, 43
STOP FEAR Coalition, 170
Storie, Steve, 42
Straus, Murray A., 13, 15, 23, 41–42,
    57
    on role of community resources,
        152
    on violence by women, 45–46
stress, as factor in domestic violence,
    108–109
Suarez, Joseph, 172
substance abuse
    as factor in domestic abuse, 109
    is overlooked in domestic violence
        field, 101–102
Sugarman, D.B., 72
support groups, 145–46
Survey of Women's Health, 21
surveys
    on gender of abusers, 13–14, 15
    on mandatory reporting
        among battered women, 139–42
        among physicians, 140
Swinford, Steven, 66

Taylor, B.G., 124
terminology, of domestic violence,
    70–71
Tiefenthaler, Jill, 55
Tutty, Leslie M., 145